FAITH IS...

The Obedient Expression of Our Love for God

Victor R. Scott

ISBN-13: 978-1-942221-09-8 (paperback)
ISBN-13: 978-1-942221-10-4 (MOBI)
ISBN-13: 978-1-942221-11-1 (EPUB)

An imprint of Scott Publishing Services
Columbus, Georgia

scottpublishingservices@gmail.com

Dedication

I dedicate this book to my daughters

A Father's Prayer

May the God of all grace draw you unto Himself. May you discover what "Faith is" and live with abandon for Him. May you come to know and experience the community of the saints of the church. May you fall in love with Jesus and be empowered by the Holy Spirit of God, now and forever, Amen.

Acknowledgments

I would like to thank Carla Leon for taking the time to read the manuscript and help in sharpening the grammar and flow of the book.

I hope this book is a benefit to all who read it. Any deficiencies in it belong to me.

Table of Contents

Acknowledgments   **5**

Table of Contents   **7**

Preface   **11**

Introduction   **13**

Investigating What It Means to Believe
Faith is NOT merely blind Trust
Faith is NOT merely an occasional practice
Faith is NOT merely produced from within

Chapter 1   **33**

Seeing the Works of God
Seeing what's there to see
God's Glory in a Blind Man
Trusting God in all things

Chapter 2   **47**

Living in the Grace of God
A Theological Detour
God Protects His Promises

Chapter 3   **59**

Rejoicing in the Mercy of God
God's Grace on Display
A Celebration Worth Having
Does God Have an Ego Problem?

Chapter 4   77

Proclaiming the Truth of God
The Wisdom of a Foolish God
The Love of God Compels Us
Proclamation is the Fruit of Conviction
A Prayer For Boldness

Chapter 5   93

Crying out to the Heart of God
A Great Gift
A Spiritual Reality

Chapter 6   103

Cultivating the Mind of God
Wonder at an All-Knowing God
The Mind of Jesus
The Promise of a Renewed Mind

Chapter 7   113

Consummating the Mission of God
The Mission of God
Completing the Complete
God Invites You Into His Plan

Chapter 8   121

Yearning for the Presence of God
A Believer's Greatest Desire
What I see Is Not What I Get
We Are Not Home Yet

Chapter 9   135

Surrendering to the Will of God
Salvation Is Not Selfish
God Suffers Because Of Sin
How Far Are You Willing To Go?

Chapter 10   143

Satisfied with the Person of God
Sin Leads to Broken Fellowship
Called To Be With God

Chapter 11   151

Standing on the Word of God
The Gospel According to Paul
1. Christ Died
2. Christ was Buried
3. Christ rose on the third day
4. All this is was done "according to the scriptures."
Nothing left to Chance

Chapter 12   167

Caring for the People of God
The Heart Of The Church
Our Love is Evidence of God
To Live is Christ
Prayer for Greater Love

Chapter 13   177

Receiving the Righteousness of God
1. Why?: "For our sake..."
2. Who?: "God made..."
3. How?: "made [Jesus] to be sin [even though Jesus]
    knew no sin..."
4. Where?: "so that in [Jesus]..."
5. What?: "we might become the Righteousness of God."
Conclusion

Chapter 14   189

Radiating the Glory of God
Dreams Of A Perfect Life
God Is The Giver Of Faith
Jesus' Desire For His Disciples

Chapter 15   **199**

Recognizing the Hand of God
    Why Are We Surprised When We Suffer?
    Some Ridiculous Verses
    Suffering May Not Be A Curse
    Opportunities Wasted
    Strive for what is better

Conclusion   **217**

An Ongoing Journey Toward Home
    The Gospel is the Call from Home

About the Author   **225**

Preface

This book has been a work in progress for several years. It started as a series of messages for my youth group. It then became a series of posts for my website. Now it is a full-fledged book.

With each iteration, more content and context was added. Each time I came back to the topics covered in these pages, the more vibrant the ideas became in my mind. My hope for this book is that as you interact with the ideas in each chapter a sharper, brighter image takes shape in your mind about this thing we call faith. That each reader will be convicted and challenged to think and talk about faith in a way that is more consistent with the Scriptures' testimony and God's expectations of us.

Faith can be a difficult concept to understand for a variety of reasons. One of my goals in writing more extensively on this topic is to share with you a new vantage point from which to look at faith. To see something old in a new way. To consider what you thought you knew about faith and having it turned right-side up.

My prayer for you is that faith becomes more than just a set of beliefs you affirm. My sincerest hope is to help infuse every fiber of your being with biblically grounded, Jesus exalting, God-glorifying faith. That when people look at you and me, they see a person convinced that there is more to this life than accumulating things. That life can be pleasing to God and satisfying to us because we have accepted and received what God revealed to us in the life of Jesus.

Victor Scott
June 2019
Columbus, Georgia

Introduction

INVESTIGATING WHAT IT MEANS TO BELIEVE

From the start, I want to establish the underlying assumption that drives this book. Faith is not an attempt to build up some inner strength or courage to believe in God or anything else. That is not how the Bible describes or defines faith nor how we arrive at a belief in God. What's more, that is not how we will talk about faith in this book.

In the Bible, faith is the result of when we encounter the Truth God has displayed in his creation or declared through revelation. After this encounter, we begin to live according to what we have learned. Most people have an easy enough time understanding the first part. It's the second that causes the most trouble. Let me describe the issue another way, faith is the journey from what we know and believe to becoming people who are willing to grapple with the implications of the Gospel of Jesus Christ and live them out in our daily lives.

I called faith the result because it is the Truth that unlocks our minds and opens our hearts to understand the commands of God. The apostle Paul pointed to this when he said there were certain ideas that could only be known by revelation. And that revelation only comes by the work of the Holy Spirit to reveal it to us.

One of the fundamental ideas of the Christian faith is that the Truth is more than just information. While there is a vital defense of the concept of "truth" as a philosophical category, within the Christian worldview, the Truth is a person, and that person is Jesus Christ. Therefore, the Christian religion holds to and promotes that every person must have a relationship with Jesus. Until this relationship is a reality we will be a struggle to make sense of faith because we will not have access to the one who is Truth.

Now that we have a clearer understanding of what we mean when we use the word Truth, it leads us to the central idea of this book. The purpose of faith is not just to believe the right things. To have the correct information. The purpose of faith is to become the right kind of person. A person conformed to the very image of Jesus, and who embodies a willing submission to the commands of God. This obedience emerges because our hearts have been changed, our minds renewed, and our love awakened by the loving example of God toward us.

When we do not conform our lives to what we have seen and heard and experienced, we are not living by faith. We are only complying with the external requirements we think we understand. However, when we put our trust and confidence in the reality of the Gospel we have heard, we ought to behave in a way that reflects that hope. Not because we have to, but because that is who we have truly become. We have been changed by the miracle of Christ in us.

While the rest of this book will flesh out this basic understanding of faith, it will be helpful to understand from the outset that when the Bible describes faith it is speaking about something real and realizable in our lives. Faith is not wishful thinking or positive thinking. Faith is real, or at least it can be if we learn what it is and what it is supposed to accomplish in our lives. If we do not allow for faith to be something real, something that any and every person can realize in their lives, then any conversation about faith becomes meaningless and futile. I believe we can avoid that conclusion. I believe faith is real and that it can provide more meaning than we could ever measure.

So, what is faith? If we are going to make sense of the question we need a reference point to start from. Faith is not something unique to religious people. Every single person born bearing the image of God has the capacity for faith. Every single person believes and puts their trust and hope in something. This book tries to answer the question about faith from a Christian perspective. The perspective of what God has revealed in the Scriptures.

The reason for this focus is two-fold: first, to help those who are not Christian understand what faith is within this framework and worldview. And second, I hope it will help Christians understand that faith is not some nebulous and difficult concept just beyond their reach. Over the years, what faith is has been made more difficult. Not because faith is difficult but because faith has been divorced from its ultimate purpose, the conforming of our identities and lives into that of Jesus'. The truly remarkable idea in the Scriptures is that faith is far simpler to understand than we may have ever believed. The problematic part of faith is knowing that we are placing our faith in the right object and then exercising faith in the right way.

A good starting point that has helped all Christians through the centuries is found in the letter to the Hebrews. In order to have a Christian understanding of faith, it would make sense to start our investigation of faith by looking at Hebrews 11: 1 and 6, and you will see why in a minute. Let's look at these verses together.

> [1] Now faith is the assurance of things hoped for, the conviction of things not seen. ... [6] And without faith it is impossible to please him, for whoever would draw near to God must believe that he exists and that he rewards those who seek him.

The essence of these two verses suggests that faith is not just about the circumstances and events of this life. It is almost as if the writer of Hebrews wanted to point us to a reality that is not even found here on earth in a tangible sense. Faith is not about the "stuff" we get when we believe in the Truth but rather about who we are becoming as we travel life's road with God.

In other words, the writer of Hebrews tells us faith is supposed to point us to realities that are not visible in the physical world and yet are just as real and true. Realities that exist on God's plane of existence—in the spiritual world. While this may be difficult to understand at first, I am persuaded we all know this intuitively. We can't see love, but when know what it is. We can't see joy, but we recognize it when we experience it. There are so many realities we can't see and yet we accept as being just as real and just as vital to the human experience. Why not faith?

Accepting the spiritual component of our existence is critical to making sense of faith, regardless of your worldview. Coming to terms with the fact that there are non-physical realities may explain why faith has been described as "things hoped for" in Christian Scriptures and theological discourse.

The inescapable fact is that what we are supposed to be hoping for is not found on this earth. We should not be trying to live our best possible life now for some temporary or temporal benefit or reward. The bottom line is that when we, as followers of Jesus are talking about faith, what we are ultimately saying is that our confidence is in what God has said and done and promised. Our trust in God should reach such heights that any physical manifestation is irrelevant because it is unneeded. That even if we do not yet have it, we live as though we did.

This passage will serve as the scriptural foundation for our understanding of what faith is throughout the rest of the book. Now, our task will be to find a way of rendering this powerful reality in a way that helps us today and every day in our lives.

I discovered some clues of how to do this after working as a youth pastor for just short of ten years. And during that time, I learned some valuable lessons about life and faith. Due to my time in youth ministry, I found that restatements of biblical truths can help facilitate how we understand what those truths mean. So, how would we restate what the writer of Hebrews said? For the remainder of this book, we will use the following restatement of the verse in Hebrews 11:

**Faith is living with the conviction
that everything God says in the Bible
is first, true, and
second, it is true for me.**

This restatement is simple and is intended to draw specific attention to the implications of Hebrews 11:1. However, before we can get there, we should take some time to make sure we understand and dispel several misconceptions regarding faith. There are three specific and significant misunderstandings about faith we have to clarify and eliminate from our minds before we can continue our discussion of what faith is. We will address them here in this introduction.

FAITH IS **NOT** MERELY BLIND TRUST

One of the most common misconceptions of faith is that it is trusting or believing in something you cannot fully know with any degree of certainty. It is often commonly described as a blind leap or, more simply, a leap of faith. The idea this description promotes is that faith, in order for it to be faith, requires some degree of ambiguity or ignorance or uncertainty. Those who categorize faith in this way imply that if faith is to be genuine, existentially satisfying, or even spiritual, it cannot be grounded in facts or reason in any meaningful way.

There is one fundamental problem with this description of faith for followers of Christ. It is not based on anything found in scripture. The faith the Bible describes and promotes is grounded in an objective reality. This object is more real and more certain than our very lives. This objective reality is the very life of God. Biblical faith is undeniably and inseparably tied to the very character and nature of God. When we divorce faith from God's character and divine nature it becomes difficult, if not impossible, to have anything resembling biblical faith. God's character is the ground, the foundation, of everything that we believe and hope for as disciples of Jesus Christ.

The writer of Hebrews asserts as much when they make the following statement describing what God declared to Abraham. After their conversation, Abraham's confidence in God's promise to make him a great nation was set and unshakable (Genesis 12:2). For the first time in Abraham's interactions with God, he understood the nature and character of the God he worshiped. Thomas Lea writes,

> "God found no one greater than himself to whom he could appeal in an oath. God's Word itself was a foundation strong enough for our trust and confidence. When God added an oath to his Word, the addition made the promise even more certain."[1]

Just like Abraham, we should make a similar evaluation of God's character. God's promises are just as sure for us who believe in them today as they were for Abraham. And the reason is that God has not and does not change. If we are going to live our lives in a manner worthy of the Gospel, we must hold to our confidence in God and his word. So, where do we find the foundation

---

[1] Thomas D. Lea, vol. 10, *Hebrews, James*, Holman New Testament Commentary (Nashville, TN: Broadman & Holman Publishers, 1999), 114.

of the promise that God made to Abraham? We find it in Hebrews 6:13.

> [13] For when God made a promise to Abraham, since he had no one greater by whom to swear, he swore by himself…

The idea of making oaths is not as common in our historical context. We do not talk about people being true to their word any longer. And this gets close to what we are looking at here. However, it is important to remember that when oaths were made during Abraham's time, the object you swore by was supposed to be something that was greater than you. So, if I wanted to prove my commitment I would say something like, "I swear by Mt. Everest that I will fulfill my part of the deal." This way, the person with whom I was making the oath would know and trust that we would abide by the conditions of the oath. So, if we understand this as an accurate way of understanding what happened in ancient times, then what does God swear by to show he will fulfill the requirements of his promises? The Greek word translated "to swear" is defined in the following way in the *Greek-English Lexicon of the New Testament*:

> …to affirm the truth of a statement by calling on a divine being to execute sanctions against a person if the statement in question is not true (in the case of a

deity taking an oath, **his divine being is regarded as validating the statement**). (emphasis added)[2]

Notice what happens when "the deity" is the one making the oath. When God is the one making claims and promises there is no reason to doubt what he says. The stipulations laid out in the oath are as good as completed from the moment the oath was made. This is an amazing proposition to consider. One we may struggle to hold on to in difficult times.

When we realize and internalize the unshakable reality that there is nothing or no one greater than God, we begin to think differently about what it means to take what God says, accepting it without reservation. In fact, when we are able to hold our doubts in check, we will be able to trust God implicitly.

God swore by Himself. Think about that. God's very character served (and continues to serve) as the basis for Abraham's confidence and for ours today. Abraham's faith in God was not blind trust in something unknown. Abraham's trust and, by extension, our trust must be based on someone who is steadfast and undeniably trustworthy. We can have confidence that God will never fail or falter. Faith, therefore, should not be described as a blind trust because faith, as the Bible describes it, is

---

[2] Johannes P. Louw and Eugene Albert Nida, vol. 1, *Greek-English Lexicon of the New Testament: Based on Semantic Domains*, electronic ed. of the 2nd edition. (New York: United Bible Societies, 1996), 440.

founded on the character of the one who made the promise, and his character is beyond reproach.

FAITH IS NOT MERELY AN OCCASIONAL PRACTICE

The second misunderstanding of faith is most easily seen when we try and describe faith in a compartmentalized way. Faith is not something **I DO** as some sort of behavior modification. When we talk about faith, we are describing someone **I have become**. (This second idea also serves as one of the foundational principles of this book.) The difference between these two positions cannot be overstated. Until we make this switch in how we think about faith, we will fail to understand why our faith "doesn't work."

Faith will never "work" when we think of it as something we possess. We must move away from thinking of faith as something I have in the same sense that we have keys or a house. Faith must become an attribute that is intrinsically a part of who we are. We need to move away from thinking of faith as a tool and begin to see faith as an attribute of our very nature. My faith is who I am.

Faith is so much more than a gimmick or some kind of magic trick. To talk about faith in these terms, even if unintentionally, is damaging to our ability to know what faith is. Faith must become the characteristic that defines and identifies who we are to the world around us, but more importantly to ourselves. If I do not see myself as a person of faith, I will continue to think that faith can be enlarged by doing various activities within the life of the church and community at large. My faith is not determined by what I do, but who I am. But what I do is undeniably informed and shaped by what I believe.

It has become trendy and even expected to speak of *personal* or *private* faith. I would like to argue there is no such thing. The tendency of the world outside the church to force this individualistic notion onto a religious conversation has been harmful to the Church. The reason is it has forced a concept foreign to the Scriptures into the consciousness of Christ-followers. While the world may want to compartmentalize the human experience, there does not exist in the Bible's understanding of the human journey any room to compartmentalize our faith from the rest of our existence. At its root, this approach to life, I believe, is a demonic tactic to isolate believers from the life-giving vine, Jesus Christ. It is designed to isolate *who we are* supposed to be in Christ from *what we do*. A privatized faith is a deception keeping us from connecting to the community of God, with whom we share a common identity in Christ.

We should take care in making jokes about something being "unchristian" and yet we proceed on laughing or participating in the activity. What this behavior exposes is that we have not made a strict connection between who we say we are in reality and the identity we say we have in Christ. This immaturity betrays our true growth and exposes us as not having fully conformed to the example of Jesus.

When we section off parts of our lives from other areas, we have not fully embraced who we are in Christ. It's that simple. We cannot have a personal life and a social life and a church life and on and on. Every aspect of our lives must be brought into submission to Christ's desires and will. The moment we give ground to anything that is not of God but can still allow it to be a part of our lives we are surrendering vital ground. We are losing in one of the most critical areas of our lives—our spiritual integrity. When we leave a door open in our understanding of faith we allow the negative influence of the world access to our lives. We even leave ourselves vulnerable to demonic distraction and distortions of the truth as contained in Scripture.

As I read the Bible, I find statements made by some of its writers to be hard to believe. The primary reason for my disbelief is that I struggle to make sense of how the reports could be true. The apostle Paul may be the Bible's best example of this. Paul makes many statements that, in some cases, would be heresy if it were not in God's word.

In the book of Galatians, Paul made an incredible claim about what it means to live a life committed entirely to God in Christ. He declares to the saints in the church of Galatia:

> [20] I have been crucified with Christ. It is no longer I who live, but Christ who lives in me. And the life I

now live in the flesh I live by faith in the Son of God,
who loved me and gave himself for me. (Galatians
2:20)

Whose life was Paul living? When was he living that life? Only on Sundays? Only when the mood struck him? I don't think so. Life is lived EVERY day. Life is lived in all kinds of circumstances, many not of our choosing. "The life I now live…" is not an occasional kind of life.

If my faith is going to be what the Bible describes, I have to see that my life has been replaced with Christ's life. Our commitment to the cause of Christ and the message of the Gospel must be total and unyielding. Until we recognize that Jesus is not interested in only living through us once or twice a week for a couple of hours, we will suffer from an anemic faith devoid of power or purpose. We will have a faith that is weak and inconsistent with the testimony of the Scripture.

We have to see our lives in a new way. We have to live our lives knowing Jesus is seeking total surrender from His followers. And why does Jesus want this surrender? So that His purposes, rather than ours, might be seen in the world!

The second misconception we have to remove from our thinking is that faith is an occasional practice. It is the steady and deliberate march toward God every single day. The journey of faith is not lived only on the mountain tops or in the valleys between them. The life of faith is lived in every step we take.

FAITH IS NOT MERELY PRODUCED FROM WITHIN

The third misconception of faith may be the most difficult to understand of the three discussed here. In order to understand what faith is, we have to see that faith is NOT produced from within. I use the word produced intentionally here. What I mean is that faith is not something that exists as a thing in itself. Faith is the byproduct of other forces at work in our lives.

Paul writes an interesting phrase regarding faith in his letter to the Roman church. Let's look at it quickly.

> So then faith *comes* by hearing, and hearing by the word of God. (Romans 10:17 NKJV)

Faith is the byproduct of two events. The first is the proclamation of the Gospel. The immediate context of this verse is of the missionary work of spreading the Gospel to those who had not yet heard it. But, why is there this need at all? Because, without the proclamation, there can be no hearing, which is the second event. Or said another way, the hearing of the preached Gospel is the primary catalyst for faith. Without the Gospel, no one can know or believe in Jesus for the forgiveness of sins. No one can know that they have been adopted into the family of God. Without the proclamation of the Gospel, no one will know that there is hope at the end of the road. So, we should understand the word "hearing" to describe the moment when the truth of God's word and the promises God has made are accepted by the hearer as true, not only in principle as some kind theoretical exercise but as a matter of personal fact.

What this means is faith is not something that exists independent of an object of faith as we have already seen. I can't just walk around "having faith." In other words, faith is not something I possess, faith is something that possesses me. Every decision and action we make reveals what we believe. Faith is always aimed at something outside of ourselves. This is why faith is not something that comes from inside. In short, my faith is triggered or activated by the object that I am putting my faith in. The Word of God preached is the spark that ignites our faith when it is accepted as the truth.

When we talk about faith we must make sure to remember that we are talking about having faith "in" something. Peter understood the nature of this when he reminded his readers about the faith they had in Jesus. This passage in 1 Peter is one of the most direct expressions we have of what faith is, and it comes from one of the original disciples of Jesus.

> [6] In this you rejoice, though now for a little while, if necessary, you have been grieved by various trials, [7] so that the tested genuineness of your faith—more precious than gold that perishes though it is tested by fire—may be found to result in praise and glory and honor at the revelation of Jesus Christ. [8] Though you have not seen him, you love him. Though you do not now see him, you believe in him and rejoice with joy that is inexpressible and filled with glory, [9] obtaining

the outcome of your faith, the salvation of your souls.
(1 Peter 1:6-9)

Peter helps us to understand that faith, if it's going to be properly called faith, must have an object. He asks, what is the "outcome of your faith"? The obvious answer is salvation. But, the question that we should be asking and trying to answer is what is that faith holding onto that produces that salvation? Peter tells us in verse 8. Faith that results in salvation comes because we trust the one we "have not seen" and yet love. If we are going to understand what faith is, we have to move beyond mere belief in ideas, concepts, philosophies, or religious platitudes. We have to move toward seeing faith as trusting in Jesus as the *object* of our faith. Without trust in the proper object, our faith will be meaningless and in vain.

Everything Jesus did, said, and continues to do through His disciples become the reasons why the world will be compelled to consider Jesus. The mission of proclaiming the Gospel to the ends of the world is the reason why the church must live up to the challenge. When we, as God's people, fail to consistently focus on Jesus, we are denying those who are looking at us the opportunity of witnessing a genuine expression of faith in Jesus. The church, as she is embodied by every faithful Christian, is the means God has chosen to communicate the Gospel to the nations. The church is God's only plan. There is no backup plan. No plan "B." God doesn't need a backup plan to accomplish his will.

It can be difficult to understand how we all are being touched by God's grace, God's people, and God's word. And, as these and other expressions of God's goodness and love are seen and felt in our lives we will find ourselves drawn closer to God. We do not come to know the faith the Bible describes when we are isolated or independent of God's chosen means. This is one of the more magnificent promises God has given to the Church. In and through the Church, God is making his appeal to the world. The Church can only fail when it forgets to trust in God to sustain it. The moment this connection of trust is severed, the Church risks the judgment of God falling upon her.

The Church must do everything it can to live into the purpose of faithfully taking the Gospel to every nation and tongue. When the church does this, the pressure to "save people" will diminish and our desire to serve God faithfully will increase. Our responsibility is to be faithful to God. We must fight the temptation to assume a role in the purposes of God that goes beyond our ability and mission.

❖❖❖❖❖❖❖❖

If we are going to know and live out what faith is, we have to know what it is **NOT**. These three misconceptions are essential to remember as we move forward. As we journey together over the next several chapters remember that faith is more than you ever imagined, it will not be less.

As followers of Jesus, we are to become for the world as he became for us. The Christian life is an incarnated life. Jesus is the model of what our own lives should now look like. Therefore, the better we understand what it means to live out the Gospel, the closer we are to reflecting faith as God conceived it and Jesus lived it.

My hope for the time you spend reading these pages is for your desire to dig into what it means to place your faith in God through Jesus will be enriched, deepened, and strengthened. This book will not attempt to make up a definition of faith that is difficult to understand and harder to live out. The purpose of this book is to make the faith of the Bible tangible and practical, to make it easier to understand and hopefully exercise. My hope is to make faith feel less like trying to hold on to thin air and more like standing on solid ground. Therefore, let's begin our journey together as we discover what faith is.

❖ ❖ ❖ ❖ ❖ ❖ ❖ ❖

[1] As he passed by, he saw a man blind from birth. [2] And his disciples asked him, "Rabbi, who sinned, this man or his parents, that he was born blind?" [3] Jesus answered, "It was not that this man sinned, or his parents, but that the works of God might be displayed in him. [4] We must work the works of him who sent me while it is day; night is coming, when no one can work. [5] As long as I am in the world, I am the light of the world."

John 9:1-5

❖ ❖ ❖ ❖ ❖ ❖ ❖ ❖

Chapter 1

FAITH IS...

SEEING THE WORKS OF GOD

Eyeglasses have been a part of my life since I was about five years old. Over the years I have gone to the optometrist on a regular basis. But, on occasion, during my appointments, the doctor will administer drops to dilate my pupils. Doing this helps the doctor examine the interior of my eyes to ensure that there are no structural changes or damage. If you have never had this done, it is an interesting experience. After the exam, it still takes a few hours before your pupils regain their ability to dilate on their own and adjust to light changes. I already have a sensitivity to light but, when my pupils cannot control the amount of light that hits the back of my eyes, I am more likely to get a migraine. There is too much light entering my eyes for the cones and rods on the back wall to process effectively.

In many ways, we all can find ourselves in a similar situation spiritually. An outside force finds its way into our lives and we can no longer control what makes its way in. When we cannot defend ourselves against spiritual attacks we become vulnerable to more pain and suffering than we ever wanted, or even thought possible.

It's interesting that Jesus used the eye to illustrate this very idea. Jesus told his disciples that the eye is the window to the soul (Matthew 6:22-23). Whatever is happening in a person's life can be traced back to the influences they are allowing into their lives. The reality of what Jesus said to his disciples should inform what we allow to pass through our eyes into our minds and hearts.

> [22] "The eye is the lamp of the body. So, if your eye is healthy, your whole body will be full of light, [23] but if your eye is bad, your whole body will be full of darkness. If then the light in you is darkness, how great is the darkness!

In the same way, our pupils are designed to protect our vision, God has given us a spiritual pupil to protect our mind and soul—it is our conscience. Our conscience helps us to gauge the moral, social, personal, and spiritual impact of our decisions. When we use our conscience, we are living and acting according to God's design. If, however, we violate our conscience, we cause injury to ourselves and potentially to others at a spiritual level. This is what I believe many in the church have failed to understand. Many of the wounds we suffer in life and in the church are spiritual in nature. Yes, the choices of others have a part to play in all of this, but our heart and our spirit are what has been damaged. That is why Jesus reminds the disciples to consider the "greatness" or depth of the darkness in a person's soul if a person's eye is dark.

This raises the following questions. First, what do we do when we can no longer see what God has put in front of us to see? Second, how do we regain control of our vision? If we are going to understand what faith is, we have to regain our ability to see as God intended. Anything short of this puts our spiritual health at risk.

SEEING WHAT'S THERE TO SEE

Too often I find myself wanting an explanation for an event or situation so that MY life will continue to make sense. I don't like it when my view of the world doesn't work out just how I wanted. This could very well be the problem, but we won't talk about that just yet. I keep looking for God to agree with me; that my view of how events should unfold is correct. The unyielding truth about the purposes and will of God is that he doesn't owe me an explanation for anything.

God tells Job just as much when Job worked up the nerve to confront God. Job wanted to let God know what he thought was unjust with what had happened to him (Job 29-31). The events of Job's life are some of the most unimaginable any one person could experience. In one day, he found out that his livestock and crops had been destroyed. Then, while still processing the loss of his livelihood (and if that were not enough), Job was then told that all of his children were killed in an accident during a party (Job 1:13-19).

If there was anyone who could curse God and have a good case for doing it, it would have been Job. But he did not do it. The story of Job is filled with twists and turns that reveal the character of the man. It is interesting that at the end of the book, after holding his ground and not calling God's character and motives into question, Job finally cracks, just a little bit, and he finally does question God about why so much suffering had taken place in his life. Job asks and ponders why the circumstances of his life were what they were. God's response to Job is one of the most direct and humility inducing in the Bible (Job 38-41). You should read the exchange for yourself.

So many times, we look at the events of our lives and believe there is too much randomness to what is happening; that our lives are just marked by chaos and little else. If this were true, life would be a series of unfortunate tragedies. While we may not always understand why something happened, we are not left to fend for ourselves regarding what God is going to do with what is taking place around us. God's faithfulness never wanes. He will fulfill his promises regardless of what we do or fail to do. The story of Job serves as a reminder that just because life throws us various curve balls, God is a just and fair judge. God will deal with each of us impartially.

When the Bible says that God is impartial it means that he makes no comparison between individuals. Not one. God deals with me without having to reference anyone else. I know this sounds simple to understand but, the truth we are considering is not just that God is good or being fair with each person. God is able to look at you and me and treat me without any bias whatsoever.

The reason God does not show any favoritism is that God does not deal with us as a group. God deals with each person individually. He deals with each of us impartially. What we have done and what others have done to us does not cause God to look at us differently. God can sift through the baggage and spiritual injuries that we have suffered and deal with our true self. It is as if God is able to treat us as if you or I were the only people on the planet. God does not let the existence of another person lead him to treat us unfairly. This is a fundamental attribute of God's nature and is therefore immutable.

This attribute also allows us to know that God can be trusted. We can know that regardless of what happens or what we do, God will interact with us in an unbiased way. While there may be times we may want him to treat us better, or others more strictly, nothing will alter God's disposition toward us. God is the only one in the entire universe who can be objective about any and everything.

GOD'S GLORY IN A BLIND MAN

The events of John 9 are interesting, provocative, and even confounding. A man is born blind. We take that for granted in our day, but during Jesus' time, this was understood as an unmistakable sign that someone had sinned. The commonly held belief was only someone guilty of some transgression would have the misfortune of being born without sight. Craig Keener notes that "Jewish teachers believed that suffering, including blindness, was often due to sin; one could suffer for one's parents' sins or even for a sin committed by mother or fetus during the pregnancy."[3]

What is striking is the notion that the man was capable of being guilty of sin *before* he was born! But, as the religious leaders assumed, if there is a causal relationship to the suffering we endure or the calamity we face, then we have a serious problem on our hands. We see this assumption articulated in the question that the Pharisees asked in John 9:2. There are many responses Jesus could have given to the question and the situation. We will look at what I think are the three most obvious.

First, Jesus could have agreed with the assumption that sin was the reason for the man's handicap. However, Jesus does not. To agree with this first assumption would have lent weight and credibility to the Pharisee's theology, and Jesus was not going to do that. Doing that

---

[3] Craig S. Keener, *The IVP Bible Background Commentary*: New Testament (Downers Grove, IL: InterVarsity Press, 1993), Jn 9:2.

would not have advanced Jesus' desire to show the world why sin is more than something to be avoided, sin must be destroyed. Merely thinking that sin could be avoided through adherence to the law and therefore all fear and concern would cease is naïve at best. The path Jesus chooses reveals the flaw in the Pharisee's world-view and sets a new direction.

Second, Jesus could have changed the direction of the conversation toward the good that would come from healing this man's handicap. Since birth, this man's parents knew the kind of life he would be resigned to live. Having to live off the benevolence of those around him would be the only way any viable existence could be carved out. Healing would have restored some dignity to this man's life. But, Jesus does not focus in on this either. Jesus was not interested in making the healing of this man the end of the story. To think Jesus would be that short-sided would put us in the position of undermining the wisdom of God. So, we must not make the same mistake ourselves.

Third, Jesus could have attempted to console the man, telling him how things will be better for him in the New Jerusalem where he would never have to worry about begging or relying on the kindness (or pity) of others to survive. Jesus did not do this either. This would have played into the misguided notion that true blessings would only come at the end of life. Each person just had to endure their lot in life until they arrived at the Promised Land.

What this option dismisses is how God's love and grace toward us as his children began in eternity past and is fulfilled in our lives, in the present. This does not mean that every wrong in life will be made right or even averted. Jesus did not want to push off into the future the reality that while all blessings will be enjoyed in their ultimate and perfect expression in God's presence, God does not wait to extend his blessings to us here on this earth. We are waiting for Jesus to return or for our time to enter heaven, but that waiting is not devoid of God's blessing. If Jesus had allowed this idea to remain unchallenged, he would have undermined God's plan for Jesus' own life, death, and resurrection.

Jesus does not choose any of these options in responding to the Pharisees' inquiry. Jesus takes a completely different approach. One that is actually unexpected to the listeners, but right in line with the way Jesus normally acted. Jesus says that *the reason* the man was born blind was so that God's works would be seen in the man! "The reason for this man's suffering was not that anyone had sinned; this man's blindness was allowed so that through his life God's glorious light might be displayed."[4] The blindness was a part of God's purpose for this man so that others might see God's work in the world, through the Son.

---

[4] Robert B. Hughes and J. Carl Laney, *Tyndale Concise Bible Commentary*, The Tyndale reference library (Wheaton, IL: Tyndale House Publishers, 2001), 475.

This can be a difficult proposition for us. How do we feel about the idea that some of what we may have to endure in life is there precisely so "God's glorious light might be displayed" in and through us? In our current cultural climate, both inside and outside the church, this would not sit well in the theologies of many people. And yet, this is precisely what Jesus is telling us. He is telling us that some of what we see in the world happens as the natural effect of original sin and not the result of individual personal sins. But God is able to use each and every situation and circumstance to bring about the fulfillment of his ultimate plan in the world and our lives. God will make his glorious light shine brightly. If we want to see it, we must reject anything that would dare to block out God's activity in the world.

TRUSTING GOD IN ALL THINGS

There are times when I wonder if I can accept as a possibility that even our trials can be used by God. That God can and does use all things to accomplish his works in the world. In the event above we see that God can truly use some of the most challenging circumstances in our lives and reveal His glory. We have to ask ourselves if we are ready to trust God in all things. Are we prepared to accept that some of the events and circumstances of our lives are a part of our experience precisely because God allowed them to unfold that way?

A significant difficulty will emerge if we are not ready to accept this. It has to do with the way we understand how God treats injustice in the world. Either God is active in and aware of everything that happens in the world or God is deficient in his governance of the world in some way. If we go with the second option, we have just made it "easier" for us to believe that bad things happen because God is somehow missing in action. This second option will eventually erode the foundation of our faith in God if it becomes the way we decide to go.

We should not attribute evil to God. God does not sin. Therefore, it is crucial to make sure our theology matches how God reveals how he works and interacts with the world. What tends to happen is in those times when we can't explain how God could use something for good, we blame God for ignoring our situation or even causing it. There are times when we find ourselves wondering if having a God who knows and works in and through everything is better than having a God who can't or doesn't? You see, if handicaps and tragedies are a part of what God takes into account to accomplish his purposes, we struggle to trust God when he doesn't just fix it or even prevent the situation from happening. God takes everything into account, including all of the craziness of the human experience and weaves his perfect will in and through it.[5] In God's wisdom, he is taking a tragedy and the presence and effects of evil into account and finds a

---

[5] In Chapter 15 we will look more intentionally at the issue of suffering and how it relates to God's activity in the world.

way to turn them for his glory and our good. That doesn't make us feel good when it's happening to us. But if we are going to consistently believe what the Bible says, we have to see God's goodness as being at work behind the scenes, even if we can't see it in or through what is happening.

The way Jesus answers the question about the reason for the man's blindness reveals that sin, while an important element in the equation and requiring of Jesus' sacrifice, is not a blip on God's radar. Jesus' answer provides us with a way of understanding why and how God acts the way He does. God is more interested in his works being seen than in our sin being pitied! Why is that? The answer is more straightforward than we might imagine. God knows that if his works are seen, his glory will be known, and his name will grow in fame throughout the whole world. And, if this happens, then we will see our sin for what it is and recognize how spiritually destitute we truly are and how great our need for God really is.

Faith is seeing the works of God for what they are, opportunities for sinful humanity to see the glory of God so we can put our trust and confidence in him. When we see the works of God we do not lose faith in God because we begin to see how everything that happens can be used by him. It is not wishful thinking. It is faith-filled knowing.

Faith requires a new "seeing." A seeing based on the character of God and the truth of his word. We must diligently look for the works of God, which are all around us. As we see God's work, how we see everything else will also change.

If anybody saw the works of God that day, it was the man who had never seen anything at all! And his testimony was one of faith, boldness, and assurance. Should our response be any different?

❖ ❖ ❖ ❖ ❖ ❖ ❖ ❖

[11] … for I have learned in whatever situation I am to be content. [12] I know how to be brought low, and I know how to abound. In any and every circumstance, I have learned the secret of facing plenty and hunger, abundance and need. [13] I can do all things through him who strengthens me.

Philippians 4:11b-13

❖ ❖ ❖ ❖ ❖ ❖ ❖ ❖

Chapter 2

FAITH IS...

LIVING IN THE GRACE OF GOD

As I thought about the title of this chapter — "Faith is Living in the Grace of God" — I could have said "by" or "with" the grace of God. But the more I thought about it, I found that my most significant challenge to being a Christian and living out the convictions and beliefs that I now hold is living **IN** what God has given. The idea that I had in mind was that the grace of God has become the atmosphere within which we exist. God's grace is not just something we have; it is actually something we are in. We are **IN** God's grace. This is why we ought to be comforted and find assurance in our relationship with God. Regardless of the circumstances, we can trust that God is near to us.

As I studied and tried to make sense of where we live as it relates to God's grace, I remembered one of Paul's more peculiar phrases (of which there are a few!). In his letter to the Colossians, Paul extolled the freedoms believers now have in Christ. There were some within the community who were trying to pull the church back into the former ways of living out their religious life (to first be good Jews and then be good Christians).

Paul was telling the Colossian Christians they were no longer bound to any particular religious festivals or dietary regulations. He encouraged them to remember how any activity that satisfies the self-righteousness of a man's heart was to be dismissed as irrelevant. In Paul's mind, the reason for the freedom all believers enjoy was due to Jesus' sacrifice and is based on a change in where we are spiritually located. Paul claimed that every follower is found in a new "where," a new position with God, as much as we are all motived to live according to a new "why" or "how." Look at the way Paul frames his reason for his confidence in Colossians 3:3:

> [3] For you have died, and your life is hidden *with* Christ *in* God. (emphasis added)

I have read this passage many times and I still can hardly believe it says what it says. If this statement is true, then we indeed can have confidence in God's promise of eternal life. We also can have confidence that when God speaks of his own faithfulness, He will follow through.

We can have unquestioning assurance that our lack of faith does not erase the work of God through Christ for us.

If we are hidden *with* Christ *in* God, then any time God does not keep a promise to us he is also hurting himself because we are "in God." As incomprehensible as this may sound, it is a consequence of our current location in God that we are in a radically new relationship with God. If we are **with** Christ, then whatever happens to him happens to us. And, if we are **in** God, every time God falters in his promises to us who have been adopted as sons and daughters, God's character can be called into question.

But, that is not all. There is another reality of our position with Jesus in God. We are not alone in our salvation. We are with Jesus. We are no longer lost, and we will never be lost again because we are right with our Savior, where he is. What safer place could there be than with Jesus?

As I have tried to make sense of this in my own journey of faith, I have discovered the difference between living in the grace of God and thinking we have the grace of God is the issue of control. Grace is about God. In every circumstance of life, God is in control. That is the most difficult reality to accept about being a disciple of Jesus. God is not interested in doing things according to our way of thinking (Isaiah 55:8-9). As a matter of fact, God has told us that our way of thinking is futile and foolish by default. God's priorities are eternally different than our own. God has no need of our counsel. Never has. When we grow in our awareness of what God's grace provides for us, we will be able to live out what our faith truly is.

A THEOLOGICAL DETOUR

While digging into theological issues is not the primary purpose of this book, a small detour will be helpful here. There are some who have asserted that a person's salvation can be "lost" if sinful behavior does not cease completely. I understand the theological and volitional reasons for this way of thinking, but there is a small (and by "small" I really mean insurmountably huge!) problem with this theological point of view. Paul's implication in Colossians 3:3 appears to indicate that when we have been given salvation as a free gift (Ephesians 2:8), the life we were living is counted and having ended and our new, current life is not even entrusted to us for safe-keeping. No, our salvation is such a precious gift God has kept it in as safe a place as he could have imagined. God has preserved our salvation within himself until we enter his presence (as we will see below).

If that were not enough, God has also entrusted our salvation into the capable hands of the one who purchased it, Jesus Christ, our Lord, Savior, and King. When Jesus died on the cross he did not fulfill the prophecies of the Old Testament and endure the injustice of a bogus trial, the shame of the cross, and a hasty burial in a borrowed grave just so we could undo everything he did with our continued sin (which, by the way, he knew would not cease until his final return).

I hope you can see how all of this multiplies the problems and difficulties in formulating an accurate and coherent theology of assurance of salvation. Too often we make the mistake of starting our theology with what matters most to us rather than with what matters most to God. Theology is about God first and foremost, and it always will be.

The apostle Peter, who among all the disciples understood that if it were up to him he would have been lost and completely cut off from Jesus, has a powerful description of salvation. He shared his understanding of what redemption looks like in his first pastoral letter. In 1 Peter 1:3-5 he writes,

> [3] Blessed be the God and Father of our Lord Jesus Christ! According to his great mercy, he has caused us to be born again to a living hope through the resurrection of Jesus Christ from the dead, [4] to an inheritance that is imperishable, undefiled, and unfading, *kept in heaven for you,* [5] who by God's power *are being guarded* through faith for a salvation ready to be revealed in the last time. (1 Peter 1:3-5, emphasis added)

This right here is a perfect description of why faith is living **IN** the grace of God. When we are exercising the kind of faith the Bible is talking about, we are saying to the world our trust and confidence is not in ourselves, not in our abilities or strengths, but in God's. Even our fears and concerns become insignificant in the grand scheme of things. The promise of God contained in Peter's words is we do not even need to be discouraged by our weaknesses. God's strength is what we are trusting in. We can trust in God to keep what he has provided because he is guarding our inheritance by his power. In my estimation, this is one of the most comforting and reassuring passages in the entire Bible. When we are no longer living in fear, trying to keep God happy, we can actually make God happy by living in a genuine and loving relationship with him.

We will look at the reality of how we are even able to live a life of greater holiness in more detail later in the book, specifically Chapter 13, where we look at *Receiving the Righteousness of God*. However, it is vitally important to underscore now that what God has done in and through the life, ministry, and the death and resurrection of Jesus cannot be undone. Once salvation is applied it cannot be removed, by us or by God. And the reason? Because God does not go back on his promises! God has never and God will never default on his grace.

This reality is the foundation of a Christian understanding of faith. Without it, the entire theological system comes crashing down upon itself. If we are going to know what it means to live in the grace of God, we have to take seriously Jesus' entire ministry—from birth to death to resurrection.

The grace of God proceeds from somewhere. And that somewhere is the very heart of God. Grace is the manifestation of God's love and holiness. If God is not gracious, then he is not God. This further underscores why understanding the role of Jesus in the salvation event is so critically important. Jesus, and everything surrounding his life, ministry, and sacrifice, is what gives cohesion and coherence to God's grace. Jesus is the bedrock upon which the foundation of faith rests. Jesus is what affects and changes us, therefore, if our theology is not Christ-centered we will never understand the fullness of God's love or the breadth of God's grace toward us. Our salvation, and Jesus' role in accomplishing it is no insignificant topic of discussion or continued reflection.

GOD PROTECTS HIS PROMISES

Now that we have made it through the detour, we can get back to the focus of this chapter. I want to help you to see what God's protection of our salvation ultimately means for us. Basically, it means that we no longer need to be distracted by what is happening around us. We should no longer be trying to do anything other than living in what God has purchased through Jesus' sacrifice, and is now safeguarding for us. What a wonderful promise.

When we know we can have confidence in everything God says, it changes how we live our lives; it changes how we pray, how we serve, and how we think about ourselves and others. We no longer need to struggle to impress God because he will never be impressed anyway. We will have a renewed awareness that we are called to a life of obedience, an obedience that is not burdened by fear.

When I consider the wonder of God's grace I am reminded of the story of "The Prodigal Son" in Luke 15. While there are three primary characters in the story, we tend to see the younger son's rebellion as the central thrust of the story. However, when we encounter the older brother, we begin to see he had parallel issues with the father's administration of the household. The story in Luke does not so much relate the story of one prodigal son, but two. Both sons failed to appreciate who the father truly was.

As the story shifts focus in the Gospel of Luke, we see one of the tenderest exchanges between two people in the Bible. The older son has returned from working and finds the "Welcome Home" party in full swing. After investigating the cause of the gathering, the elder son becomes indignant and will not even enter the premises. The father has to come out of the house to greet his first-born son. The father's words to his eldest son, his stay-at-home rebel, are so moving. Jesus puts these words in the mouth of the man:

> [31] "'My son,' the father said, 'you are always with me, and everything I have is yours. (Luke 15:31 NIV)

Just read that last phrase again: "everything I have is yours." That phrase challenges me to evaluate if I too have taken God's grace and love for granted at times as well. Have I missed what God has put on display for me to see and enjoy? A gift that is always with me, not locked up in a chest away from me. Do I not see how everything God gave to Jesus, God also has given to me because of Jesus? And, because God loves me so much he retains control of how to protect this precious gift of salvation by his power for my sake?

The fact that God does not trust me with keeping my own salvation intact is not an insult to me. It is a reason for hope, confidence, and rejoicing. It should comfort us to know that God will not allow anything to rob us of our inheritance. We have to stop trying to earn what is already ours, the same way the older brother tried to do. I have to learn how to live **IN** the grace of God. That is what the father was trying to remind his son of. "You are always with me." You are here in my house, under my roof, able to enjoy all that I have because, as a loving father, I will never keep anything from you that I have secured for you. This is the power of faith. **Faith does not seek to acquire through work what God has given in love.**

We are talking about a **COMPLETED** work of salvation. Just because we have not reached the end of the road does not mean God has changed his mind about what he has promised and done in our lives through Jesus. The majesty of the Gospel is that God did not leave the outcome up to chance. God has ensured that what he started he will see to its proper and glorious end (Philippians 1:6). Our salvation is secure, not because of anything I have done or could do. It is protected because the one who purchased it will never allow his promises to fail. The eternal treasury of God's grace will never be overdrawn and can never default. When we recognize this truth and it penetrates our minds and hearts, we will begin to experience what it means that faith truly is living IN the grace of God.

◈ ◈ ◈ ◈ ◈ ◈ ◈ ◈

[6] The Lord works righteousness
  and justice for all who are oppressed.

[7] He made known his ways to Moses,
  his acts to the people of Israel.

[8] The Lord is merciful and gracious,
  slow to anger and abounding in steadfast love.

[9] He will not always chide,
  nor will he keep his anger forever.

[10] He does not deal with us according to our sins,
  nor repay us according to our iniquities.

[11] For as high as the heavens are above the earth,
  so great is his steadfast love toward those who fear
  him;

[12] as far as the east is from the west,
  so far does he remove our transgressions from us.

[13] As a father shows compassion to his children,
  so the Lord shows compassion to those who fear
  him.

[14] For he knows our frame;
  he remembers that we are dust.

Psalm 103:6-14 (emphasis added)

◈ ◈ ◈ ◈ ◈ ◈ ◈ ◈

Chapter 3

FAITH IS...

REJOICING IN THE MERCY OF GOD

Do you remember what you felt when you realized what the implications of God's grace were for your life? How did you feel as you were awakened to the reality of what God's love meant for you? Or, do you still struggle with what we looked at in the previous chapter, living in the grace of God? As we move through the various facets of the diamond of faith, we must ask ourselves some tough questions. One of those questions is this: *Does my faith reflect an understanding of each of the characteristics described so far?* Or are you hoping to get to it "when you have more time"? I would like to tell you, if you don't already know it, the longer we procrastinate in engaging our faith and turning to God, the harder it is to do. The challenge of genuine faith is finding a way to move beyond "trying to act" like Christians and seeing our lives from an all-encompassing identity as Christians.

If we have confessed our faith in the ministry and salvation work of Jesus, then we are Christians. We are not almost Christians. We have been adopted into the family of God, and what's more, we belong to God in total. Sometimes we have a hard time making sense of what all of this means. However, that does not change this new reality. We are Christians because we are now identified with Christ. What we have not done yet is gone through the process of conforming every area of our lives to this new identity. That is a serious challenge; one that many do not take seriously enough in their lives. One that many recognize will require a lifetime of effort.

The opening question of this chapter was if you recalled the first time you truly realized what grace really was. I am not asking if you remembered what others said that it was. If we are going to make progress on this journey of faith, we have to move toward a mode of living where we interact with God based on our own personal and actual experiences. Someone else's experiences are not sufficient. We all will be required to stand before God for ourselves.

The miracle the Gospel proclaims is that in spite of this solitary requirement we will not have to stand by ourselves. Jesus is our advocate according to John's first letter (1 John 2:2). Jesus will stand with us if we stood with and for him in our lives (Matthew 10:23). This is a sobering truth. Let it sink in. Meditate on it for a moment before continuing to read.

I will tell you where I was. I was a young, seventeen-year-old kid who had just finished cussing at his dad. I was angry and hurt because I thought my father would not be proud of me if I was not a baseball player like my two younger brothers. I loved the game (I still do), I just did not have the tenacity that my brothers shared to stick with it. As soon as I said what I said, I knew I had crossed the line. I had made a decision and could not take it back. The next few moments were filled with a palpable tension. I did not know how my father was going to react. We had never been here before in our relationship. We were in unknown territory; in uncharted waters.

So, I waited for what seemed like an eternity trying to prepare myself for my dad's response. He did not yell, get angry, or even acknowledge that I had just cussed at him. He simply told me he was proud of me for who I was and that whatever I decided to do with my life was fine with him. My playing baseball or not playing baseball did not determine how he felt for me. I was his son and that was enough.

Of all the responses I expected, that was not one of them. I was utterly deflated and yet I have never felt more loved and accepted in my life. I had experienced the other side of grace. I had just experienced mercy. What I deserved and should have received was to be punished for my insolence and blatant disrespect. But, what I saw in my dad was the power of grace to rise above an insult and extend love.

GOD'S GRACE ON DISPLAY

Psalm 103 is one of the many places in the Bible where we are confronted with an unrelenting truth about God and the way he works in the world. Grace has commonly been defined and understood as God's unmerited (undeserved) favor toward sinners. This favor comes within a specific framework. It is given freely to those who accept God's invitation to have fellowship with him. Craig Keener provides some insight into the context for this invitation. "In the New Testament, [grace] generally represents the Old Testament concept of God's covenant love."[6] Throughout the entire Bible, God has consistently and continually invited all who are willing to have a relationship with him to come.

I want to take a moment and say that God's grace is not merely a sentimentality toward sinners. God is gracious because that is who he is, by nature. Grace is one of the defining characteristics of God's essential being (holiness being the other). God gives grace because without it he would not be God! God does not need any other reason to be gracious than to satisfy his own prerogative as God.

---

[6] Craig S. Keener, *The IVP Bible Background Commentary: New Testament* (Downers Grove, IL: InterVarsity Press, 1993).

Grace is what God extends toward us when what we deserve is something different. The words that should describe a human's relationship with God are judgment, wrath, and condemnation, to name a few found in the Scriptures. But, this is not what we experience. What we experience is a miracle called grace. Grace is what God has given us in the exchange at the cross. But at the moment of salvation, grace is not the only thing God has given to every penitent sinner. Mercy is also extended, and mercy is something altogether different in purpose from grace.

We no longer talk about mercy in our modern culture because it is perceived as weakness. And in the church, we don't talk about it because we are afraid to speak of sin. We are so scared to admit to ourselves or call others to take a long, hard look in the mirror. We don't even want to consider that the very reason Jesus had to die was because we, each and every person on the earth born and yet unborn, are guilty of sin. And, it is this guilt that had to be atoned for by Jesus' death on the cross.

What's even more striking to this aversion to talking about mercy, because of what it implies, is that, particularly in the western world, we have an inflated sense of justice. It would not be a stretch to say that in practice it should be called vengeance. We have formalized ways of exacting revenge rather than seeking justice for the victims. This has made the judicial process a weapon rather than a deterrent. But that is subject for another time.

The relationship between a flawed understanding of justice and mercy is this, neither can occur when the purposes are selfish and divorced from God's character. The sad state of affairs in the modern church is that mercy has morphed into all manner of benevolence ministries rather than what it was truly meant to be, a means of bringing sinners to a reconciled relationship with God. Biblical mercy has more to do with evangelism than with acts of kindness to those in need. The irony of this entire situation is that mercy is supposed to be one of the primary characteristics of God's people (Matthew 9:13) and yet we have forgotten its function with the life of Christ's people. Therefore, it would make sense then to reacquaint ourselves with a biblical understanding of mercy.

Mercy is different from grace. The primary reason is that when God extends his mercy, God is withholding from us *exactly* what we do in fact deserve. Don't miss that. There is something we all are guilty of and should be judged for. We are tainted, perverted, and polluted by sin. No one escapes. Every person is born a sinner. When we fail to understand this, we run the risk of not appreciating and even dismissing God's acts of mercy in our lives.

Some believe in the idea there are "innocent" people in the world. The truth is that that person has never truly existed. He is the figment of our corrupted imaginations. The only one to who could ever claim to be innocent of any and all sin and who walked on the earth was Jesus. The notion of an honest and pure person is one of the most blatant, delusional fantasies of the human experience. But it is one that never seems to die. We all want to believe it could be us. To think otherwise would mean accepting something about ourselves we all would rather pretend is not true.

What does all of this have to do with God's mercy? It's actually quite simple. The *Holman Illustrated Bible Dictionary* provides this explanation of God's mercy and how it relates to us as sinners.

> Mercy as given by God is the foundation of forgiveness. It is His faithfulness and steadfast love. God is not seen as displaying an emotion called mercy but as taking merciful action. ... Mercy has never been the benefit of God's people because of their merit but is always the gift of God.[7]

Only someone who accepts the reality of their sinful nature can recognize and appreciate mercy. If we do not acknowledge the first, we can never experience the second.

As we grow in our understanding of faith, we will discover why faith leads us to **REJOICING** in the mercy of God. Until we arrive at this understanding, where we can see what we have been saved from, we will struggle to rejoice in God's mercy toward us. We may have never considered it, but it takes effort to rejoice in God's mercy.

---

[7] *Holman Illustrated Bible Dictionary*, ed. Chad Brand, Charles Draper, Archie England et al. (Nashville, TN: Holman Bible Publishers, 2003), 1106.

Too often we forget we are sinners. We may be saved, but we are still sinners. We've become disconnected from any sense that we still are susceptible to sin to the point we start thinking and believing we are okay. As long as we live on this earth, with its flaws, faults, and enticements, we will be susceptible to sinning.

Rejoicing in God's mercy begins with reminding ourselves of the reasons for why we needed his mercy in the first place. The beauty of God's mercy is how when we rejoice in it, we regain the perspective we need to live in accord with God's will and character. God's mercy helps us to see we are no longer held captives by sin, even though we will struggle with the temptation to keep on sinning until Christ's return.

A Celebration Worth Having

The first time I truly made the connection and understood God's mercy was something worth rejoicing in, I was reading and studying through the apostle John's first letter. In 1 John 2:1-2, John is trying to help his readers understand the security and comfort that comes from Jesus standing as our advocate, our lawyer, in God's court. As I read these words I was struck by the tenderness with which John wrote them.

> [1] My little children, I am writing these things to you so that you may not sin. But if anyone does sin, we have an advocate with the Father, Jesus Christ the righteous. [2] **He is the propitiation for our sins**, and

not for ours only but also for the sins of the whole world. (emphasis added)

Right there, in the second verse, we find this amazing and revealing reason for our rejoicing. Jesus is our **PROPITIATION**. You should be jumping up and down at that! If you are not, don't worry. I didn't either the first time I encountered this word. It wasn't until I understood what it meant that I made the important connection between my salvation and God's mercy.

Propitiation is one of those words that is not used very much anymore in the church (if at all). And it should be. It has been translated in some versions of the Bible as an "atoning sacrifice" or "the sacrifice for our sins." While it is technically an acceptable translation, there is one significant problem with rendering the Greek word found in 1 John 2:2 in this way. That reason is that it masks the nature of Jesus' sacrificial work when he died for our sins on the cross. One of the most important components of what Jesus did for us is overlooked and perilously deemphasized.

To make sense of the word, we have to understand the various aspects of Jesus' salvific work. When Jesus died, he atoned for; he took the blemish of my sin from me by dying on the cross. If you have been in church for any length of time, you understand this as the central motif of the Gospel message. In the crucifixion, we find the ultimate fulfillment of the sacrificial system of the Old Testament (Hebrews 10:1-18). What we must not miss is when Jesus was crucified and killed a transfer took place. My sins were put on Jesus in such a way that he became guilty **FOR** my sin–and the sins of the whole world! And I, and all who believe in Jesus, have had his righteousness applied to our account, thereby erasing the penalty of sin. This can be described but never fully explained. It is a mystery of divine proportions. This exchange, at its core, is the essential understanding of atonement that is usually forgotten or diminished when speaking about Jesus' saving work on the cross. If this exchange does not take place, salvation is an empty and pitiable promise.

L. L. Morris helps us to understand why the word and idea of propitiation has lost some of its prominence in the church's lexicon.

> Propitiation properly signifies the removal of wrath by the offering of a gift. ... In modern times the whole idea of propitiation has been strongly criticized as savouring [sic] of unworthy ideas of God. Many suggest that the term 'propitiation' should be abandoned in favour [sic] of expiation, and this is done, for example, in [the Revised Standard Version].
>
> The objection to propitiation arises largely from an objection to the whole idea of the wrath of God, which many exponents of this view relegate to the status of an archaism.[8]

---

[8] L. L. Morris, "Propitiation" In , in *New Bible Dictionary*, ed. D. R. W. Wood, I. H. Marshall, A. R. Millard et al., 3rd ed. (Leicester, England; Downers Grove, IL: InterVarsity Press, 1996), 975.

The contemporary culture's dislike and even disdain for the idea of God having wrath has moved any discussion of propitiation to the theological fringe. This is a terribly sad circumstance. In light of this, a larger issue is raised. My father has often said, "Words have meaning. Therefore, know the meaning of words." This simple axiom has forced me to confront and address the reality that what a word means, many times, will force me to alter and conform my beliefs, attitudes, and behaviors to its implications. This is precisely the problem with the propitiation-expiation substitution described by Morris above. Morris again provides a clear rationale for not allowing this substitution to take place.

> Objection is made to 'propitiation' on the ground that it means the appeasement of an angry God, an idea not found in Scripture. Therefore expiation is substituted for it. But the matter is not so simple. Expiation properly has a thing as its object. We may expiate a crime, or a sin. Propitiation is a personal word. We propitiate a person rather than a sin (though we should not overlook the fact that in the Bible 'propitiate' is occasionally found with sin as the object, the meaning being 'to make propitiation with respect to sin'). If we are to think of our relationship to God as basically personal we cannot afford to dispense with the concept of propitiation. Those who advocate the use of expiation must face questions like: Why should sin be expiated? What are the consequences if no expiation takes place? Is the hand of God in those consequences? Expiation is a valuable word only if we can confidently answer 'No' to the

last question. If sin is a thing, and can be dealt with as a thing, blotted out, cast from us, and the like, then we may properly talk of expiation. But if sin affects man's relationship with God, if the relationship with God is the primary thing, then it is difficult to see how expiation is adequate. Once we bring in the category of the personal we need some such term as propitiation.[9]

An undeniable fact of the Scripture's testimony is that my sin and the sin of all of humanity is an extremely personal offense to God. To deny the personal nature of sin is to diminish both God's personhood as well as that of all people. Our sin must be propitiated because the one offended has, in fact, experienced an offense, namely our sin. The *Pocket Dictionary of Theological Terms* highlights the issue in this way,

"Biblical scholars debate whether the Greek terms deriving from *hilaskomai* should be translated as 'propitiation,' denoting the turning away of divine wrath, or, in contrast, as 'expiation,' denoting the sense of covering sins or canceling a debt."[10]

Regardless of the reasons for debating how to translate the Greek word, and regardless of the discomfort the notion of God having and expressing wrath may be to

---

[9] L. L. Morris, "Expiation" In , in *New Bible Dictionary*, ed. D. R. W. Wood, I. H. Marshall, A. R. Millard et al., 3rd ed. (Leicester, England; Downers Grove, IL: InterVarsity Press, 1996), 353.

[10] Stanley Grenz, David Guretzki, and Cherith Fee Nordling, *Pocket Dictionary of Theological Terms* (Downers Grove, IL: InterVarsity Press, 1999), 50.

some, the fullness of what Jesus did should be expressed in the Scriptures as clearly as possible. Every effort should be made to illuminate the reality of what God the Father, God the Son, and the God the Holy Spirit were accomplishing in salvation, so it is clearly understood by the reader. When we don't know the whole story, we risk basing our faith, lives, and decisions on too little information. Doing this will most assuredly lead to grave errors and devastating disappointments. Why risk these possibilities?

Jesus did indeed pay the price for our sin with the shedding of his blood. But, the act of propitiation has another tertiary idea included, though no less important. When Jesus atoned for our sin, he also gave us something that we could not acquire for ourselves.[11]

When Jesus was crucified on the cross for our sin, God pronounced judgment on all sin, for all time. At the moment of Jesus' death, God unleashed the unrestrained fury of his wrath against sin upon his Son. Let that sink in for just a minute. You may need to read that sentence again!

God did not hold any of his wrath back in reserve so he would have something left to use on us later. God has judged sin once and for all and has forgiven repentant sinners who accept Jesus' sacrifice. God did not hold anything back nor is he keeping any of his wrath toward sin in reserve to hold it over us.

---

[11] We will explore this further in the chapter about imputed righteousness in Chapter 13.

I want the following statement to sink in: **In the death of Jesus on the cross, God has finished punishing sin.** Do not miss this. God has done all of the punishing he is going to do for the sins of mankind. What is missing, what is yet left undone is the final application of the punishment to those who never accept Jesus as Lord and Savior. You see, in order for me, or anyone to receive God's grace Jesus had to die in our place. And, in order for me to experience God's mercy God had to pass my judgment onto Jesus and apply Jesus' righteousness to me.

DOES GOD HAVE AN EGO PROBLEM?

God's holy contempt of sin and the application of his just wrath against our sin had to be dealt with. This is why a propitiatory sacrifice was needed in the first place. Now, if we are not careful in describing the severity of the effects of sin, we can make it sound like God has an ego problem. If we describe it as though God has to be pacified because he was offended, we will have completely misunderstood the situation. This would be a terribly shortsighted way of seeing what took place at Calvary and what God himself was working to accomplish in and through Jesus' ministry.

The problem is not that God's ego was bruised by sin, but that God's very character was besmirched by humanity's insolent disobedience. When sin entered the world through human rebellion against God's command, humanity put God on notice and attempted a *coup d'état* against the reign of God. Obviously, this effort to dethrone God failed, however, it meant the parties involved had to be dealt with.

What makes this entire affair of sin and judgement so difficult to process is that we don't want to admit how bad the situation is! We must keep continually in mind that the right to demand restitution and the nature of punishment is never determined by the offender. Even in our flawed and broken human justice systems, we try to find a punishment that "fits the crime." And many times in western societies, that punishment is determined by a jury of peers who weigh and evaluate the evidence presented during a formal trial.

So, what then is the proper punishment for offending an eternal, holy, and pure God? Is it not an eternal, profane, and despicable hell? When my simple sensibilities are wounded, I want retribution. But, when God is the one offended, somehow God should not seek recompense. Why not? "God is gracious," some will say. "God is good," others will argue. "God is love," comes the reply. But, God's goodness, grace, and love are expressions of another more basic reality of God's being and character—God is holy.

Jesus stands between us and a holy God, and He received and endured the full thrust of God's penetrating wrath. When this truth breaches our obstinate minds and touches your sin-seared soul; when the weight of Jesus' sacrifice sits firmly on our hearts…then we will be changed. We cannot continue living and working and attending church as if what Jesus did was just something to be thankful for and then dismiss it from thought the rest of the week. No, worship is the only proper response to Jesus being our propitiating sacrifice to God's wrath.

Only when we appreciate what God should have done to us because of our sin will we rejoice in God's mercy toward us. When we understand how wretched and wicked our sin truly is, at that moment we will begin to see that mercy is also an extension of grace. Only a loving and gracious God could delay his well-deserved day in court and extend mercy to wretched and depraved sinners.

This is exactly what the apostle Paul was pointing to when he said that God put Jesus "forward as a propitiation by his blood, to be received by faith. This was to show God's righteousness, because *in his divine forbearance* he had passed over former sins" (Romans 3:25 emphasis added). God does not ignore sin. God punishes sin. But in his grace, God has also made provision to remove the penalty of sin from sinners. To make sons out of slaves; saints out of sinners; and princes and heirs to the kingdom from the paupers of the world.

Faith is rejoicing in the Mercy of God. When we are able to allow the wonder of this truth and reality of our relationship with God to be magnified in our hearts and minds, our journey of faith will be transformed. God's salvation of a lost sinner is a miracle of eternal proportions. This is what makes it a reason to rejoice. I would encourage you to give God thanks today for his mercy. Do not miss another chance to do it.

❖ ❖ ❖ ❖ ❖ ❖ ❖ ❖

¹⁸ For the word of the cross is folly to those who are perishing, but to us who are being saved it is the power of God. ¹⁹ For it is written,

"I will destroy the wisdom of the wise, and the discernment of the discerning I will thwart."

²⁰ Where is the one who is wise? Where is the scribe? Where is the debater of this age? Has not God made foolish the wisdom of the world? ²¹ For since, in the wisdom of God, the world did not know God through wisdom, it pleased God *through the folly of what we preach* to save those who believe. ²² For Jews demand signs and Greeks seek wisdom, ²³ but we preach Christ crucified, a stumbling block to Jews and folly to Gentiles, ²⁴ but to those who are called, both Jews and Greeks, Christ the power of God and the wisdom of God. ²⁵ For the foolishness of God is wiser than men, and the weakness of God is stronger than men.

1 Corinthians 1:18-25 (emphasis added)

❖ ❖ ❖ ❖ ❖ ❖ ❖ ❖

Chapter 4

FAITH IS...

PROCLAIMING THE TRUTH OF GOD

My second year of youth ministry was an interesting mixture of frustration and enlightenment. It was frustrating because I was serving in a ministry area that I vowed I never would. In spite of that, over the course of about five months, God revealed some important truths related to both youth ministry in general and my faith journey in particular. God used the experiences of that year to solidify many of the convictions I now hold.

In the fall of that year, the church I was serving at the time went on a ski trip to an outdoor wilderness camp in North Carolina. The mountains were beautiful to behold. We spent two and a half days there, during which we attended four or five services, morning and evening. The worship was great. The counselors could not have done a better job. The only point of contention I had was the subject selected by the speaker. Every single time during our meetings there, he spoke about the Gospel of Jesus. By Saturday evening I was totally frustrated. The perplexing part is I wasn't sure why. Let me explain.

Part of my frustration stemmed from the fact I did not bring my CHRISTIAN youth group to a Christian camp to be preached at like they were lost heathens destined for hell! I was bothered by the presumption of the speaker. On that weekend, I came face-to-face with a life altering realization; a profound truth that has affected the trajectory of my life and ministry since. My foundational philosophy for ministry has not been the same ever since.

What I learned, and became convinced of, was that the faithful preaching of the Gospel's simple message changes everything, and every believer should cherish every opportunity to hear that Good News. The Gospel should never become old news. Every time we hear the Gospel we should be inspired by the message because it points us to the Messiah it proclaims. The Messiah who saved us and keeps us.

Over the course of our trip, I realized that I was one of the people Paul was referring to in 1 Corinthians 1:18-22, the passage at the start of this chapter, and I vowed to never again take for granted any presentation of the Gospel. I have learned to rejoice at every time a preacher, Sunday school teacher, or fellow believer communicates how the message of Jesus has transformed their lives. Because it is the same message that changed mine. This is why Paul's letter reads more like a testimony than an academic lecture. Paul remembered what it was like to struggle and be joyously overcome by the message of the Gospel of Jesus Christ.

THE WISDOM OF A FOOLISH GOD

I have always found Paul's statement in First Corinthians (mentioned above) regarding God's wisdom to be mind-boggling. Paul essentially says that God in his most "foolish" moments is wiser than humanity's entire wisdom put together. I know this is a classic overstatement by Paul, and yet I wonder at times if Paul was not also trying to expose and reveal the hubris of the human heart.

An easy temptation as knew believers, or even for believers who have been walking with Jesus for a while, when we read the scripture is to try and find some hidden truth. Something that has been lying within the pages of God's word undiscovered by anybody else. Every once in a while, we will find something that shakes us, that enlightens us, that challenges us. It will feel new and exciting, but it has been there the whole time. We just were not ready to see it until we finally did.

The danger comes when we think we have uncovered some secret or hidden nugget of wisdom from God's eternal treasure trove; that just because some new idea has entered our heads, we have unlocked and somehow entered some realm of spiritual enlightenment.

One of the more damaging temptations we face in life is desiring access to some information no one else or very few people know about. This may be the single greatest danger in attempting to analyze or explain what is only meant to be proclaimed. Let me explain.

I was introduced to Dr. John Piper when I attended Georgia Southern University. He has a way of saying difficult things in understandable ways. I remember listening to one of Dr. Piper's sermons on Romans 9. He was speaking of the time when he began to understand, to truly grasp, what it meant for God to be sovereign in all things. You don't have to completely agree with Dr. Piper's theology to appreciate the emotional impact of what he learned. I find his recollection compelling.

> "As I studied Romans 9 day after day, I began to see a God so majestic and so free and so absolutely sovereign that my analysis merged into worship and the Lord said, in effect, *"I will not simply be analyzed, I will be adored. I will not simply be pondered, I will be proclaimed. My sovereignty is not simply to be scrutinized, it is to be heralded. It is not grist for the mill of controversy, it is gospel for sinners who know that their only hope is the sovereign triumph of God's grace over their rebellious will."*[12]

---

[12] http://www.desiringgod.org/resource-library/sermons/the-absolute-sovereignty-of-god-what-is-romans-nine-about, (emphasis added), accessed February 15, 2019.

Do you get a sense of the shift Dr. Piper experienced? One of the great lessons I have learned from Dr. Piper is that theology is not the enemy of doxology. Our study of God should not get in the way of our worship. As a matter of fact, the more deeply we study who God is the more it should help us to worship more sincerely because we see God more clearly. We should not shun deep thinking about God. We should be afraid of shallow thinking that relies on emotional tricks rather than heart-felt, heart-transforming, heart-convicting devotion.

What a beautiful description of the intersection of heart and mind in the act of worship. This is what it means for faith to be exemplified in and through the proclamation of the truth of God. As we are confronted with the truth of God—that in Christ we have new life and we who were enemies of God now have access to the mercy seat of God's grace—we will begin to recognize that the Gospel is not to be merely understood. This truth must be experienced. This is the nature of freedom inducing truth. The truth sets us free (John 8:32). This is what Jesus said. But, he never went into the details of why it sets us free or how the truth sets us free. Jesus plainly stated that this is the effect of truth in our lives.

It was the apostle Paul who took this reality and gave it structure. The apostle wanted to help his readers understand the extent and power of this freedom. All throughout his letters, Paul calls us to have the mind of Christ, to have our minds renewed, to not have our thinking conformed to the patterns of this world.

In the same way that food is processed in the stomach, the truth is processed in the mind. While food produces energy for our bodies, it is the truth that unlocks the mind from falsehood. It is the truth that produces faith in us because it gives us the categories we need to make sense of the world in which we live. It is Truth, that which is contained in the message of the Gospel and codified in the pages of the Scriptures, that enlightens and liberates, and both take place at the same time.

In light of all of this I have a question: why do we fight so hard to understand, when what God has asked is for us to enjoy? We want to dissect the truth rather than delight in what the truth is pointing too. I believe that at the root of this attitude is a misunderstanding of God's love. I could say that it is because of an ungrateful heart, but this would not be accurate. The truth is, it is difficult to be grateful when you don't understand what you are supposed to be thankful for. Or, that you should be grateful at all.

Over the years I have had the uneasy feeling that Christianity has been devolving steadily into a cultural religion and we, its adherents, have grown increasingly complacent about countering this trend. Many in the Church have gotten used to simply participating in the practice of a religious life. There is no longer an expectation among the faithful to uphold the tenets of the faith. The reasons are many, but the source is the same. The truth has not penetrated as deeply as it should. The truth has been rebuffed and redefined to suite the whims of sinners rather than to submit to the will of God.

Whether intentionally neglected or innocently overlooked, there is a sadness in my heart at the thought of the Church giving away ground to lies. When more and more people no longer feel the conviction the truth produces, the end is easy to predict. Without truth we will all go astray. We will be lost in the maze of worldly deceptions. We will be blinded by the fog of worldly philosophy and we will succumb to the malaise of lukewarm religion.

What the Church declares as its purpose is something to be adhered to. But too many are sounding the retreat on too many fronts. The American church has become so comfortable that it fails to see its self-righteous outbursts against the "restrictions" of the faith as the spiritual tantrums they have become. Only a spoiled child could look at the perfect gift of the Gospel and ask for more.

Paul in his letter to the Roman church says these simple and yet amazing words.

> [14] How then will they call on him in whom they have not believed? And how are they to believe in him of whom they have never heard? And how are they to hear without someone preaching? [15] And how are they to preach unless they are sent? As it is written, "How beautiful are the feet of those who preach the good news!" [16] But they have not all obeyed the gospel. For Isaiah says, "Lord, who has believed what

he has heard from us?" [17] So faith comes from hearing, and *hearing through the word of Christ*. (Romans 10:14-17, emphasis added)

At the heart of the Christian faith is a story that must be told. The Gospel is the story of a miraculous birth and of lives transformed. The Gospel does not need to be defended as much as displayed. It is in the telling of the Gospel that new life is born in the hearts and minds of sinners. We should not be surprised by this. Stories stimulate us to think beyond the here and now. Stories transport us to faraway places and help us to consider and contemplate differing perspectives and entertain possibilities too difficult, dangerous, or even child-like in nature. The Truth of God must be proclaimed. It is our responsibility, as followers of Jesus, to go into the world and proclaim the Good News to anyone and everyone we encounter as we travel along the way.

THE LOVE OF GOD COMPELS US

Jesus' story is the foundational reality of why, if we claim to belong to Jesus, we must make it our mission to proclaim God's truth. Our awareness and growing dependence upon Jesus is what should drive us forward with an ever-growing boldness. There is something different in us, now that we have come to know the Son of God. If this does not describe you, then stop and take some time to think about why not. The Gospel works in us the desire to share what we have received. When this desire is not present, the Gospel's effects have been short circuited at some point in our spiritual development. What then, should we be looking for?

Paul again captures for us the motivation that drives the missionary and evangelistic zeal of the church of Jesus Christ. Look how he describes it to the Corinthian church.

> [14] For Christ's love compels us, *because we are convinced* that one died for all, and therefore all died. [15] And he died for all, that those who live should no longer live for themselves but for him who died for them and was raised again. … [18] All this is from God, who reconciled us to himself through Christ and gave us the ministry of reconciliation: [19] that God was reconciling the world to himself in Christ, not counting men's sins against them. And *he has committed to us the message of reconciliation.* [20] We are therefore Christ's ambassadors, as though God were making his appeal through us. *We implore you on Christ's behalf: Be reconciled to God.* [21] God made him who had no sin to be sin for us, so that in him we might become the righteousness of God. (2 Corinthians 5:14-15, 18-21, emphasis added)

I may be overstating it, but it feels like many today within the church do not feel the compelling power of the Gospel. We have grown accustomed to its words but have failed to accept its meaning. I would have thought that something resembling the current state of affairs would never come; however, the modern expression of the church is succumbing to this every-encroaching tendency toward complacency. We have lost sight of the Gospel's purpose. We have looked upon the broken and battered body of the Lamb of God and found it trivial and mundane and unmoving. A possible reason for this disconnect is that we have failed, as a church, to clearly and consistently declare the following truth:

> **The cross is a compelling reality,
> not because Jesus was nailed to it,
> but because I wasn't.**

He hangs in my place and yours. He suffered, died, and was resurrected for you and me. To be confronted with this truth, this reality and then to shrug our shoulders is blasphemy—taking the acts of God and dismissing them as demonic, insignificant or nothing at all.

PROCLAMATION IS THE FRUIT OF CONVICTION

As I have sought to live out my faith in every area of life and through many conversations with other believers, I have discovered a common theme. Many Christians do not share the truth of God because they do not feel they have been fully transformed by the truth they received. Therefore, the thinking goes, they are not qualified to share the Gospel with others. This could not be further from the truth. Just because we are in our own process toward maturity does not disqualify us from sharing what we have seen and heard thus far on our journey.

Over the years as I have explored my own heart, I found out how easy it is to not cultivate a conviction for the truth of God. I am not talking about struggling to believe that there is a God or even that he has spoken. There are many religions that have similar truth-claims regarding the divine. The problem for these other religions and philosophical systems is that the truth they proclaim is not rooted in the character of God. This is an important distinction because Christianity is not merely pointing to or making assertions about what is "already there." The Christian faith is making specific and peculiar claims about the nature and character of the God it proclaims to be present and active in the universe. For the Christian believer, the truth is grounded in a transcendent "who" and not merely in discerning the presence of an immanent "what."

In the end, this is the fundamental difference between the faith of Jesus and the other religions of the world. Truth is not merely an idea or a philosophy or a pattern of living within biblical theology. For the Christian faith, Truth is a person. To believe in the truth is to believe in Jesus. This is the mystery and paradox of biblical religion. No other religious leader makes this claim. No other religion, ancient or modern, has ever vested that much influence in any one person. That is, except Christianity.

Jesus is the truth because everything that he said and did is true. But, that is not going far enough. Jesus is the

Truth because he is the incarnate word (John 1:1). In Jesus, truth walked on human feet, served and healed with human hands, loved with a human heart and ultimately died a human death. This is the single most unique claim in the history of religious thought. There is no comparable claim. Nothing even comes close.

Therefore, we must make it our life's aim to proclaim the story and life of Jesus. In communicating this message, we are proclaiming the truth of God. There is no higher truth to spread throughout the whole world. There is no greater endeavor to which we can dedicate our lives. There is no cause more worthy of our best efforts. Truth is not just something for which we must learn to live. Truth must become something for which we are willing to pay the ultimate price! Dr. Martin Luther King understood this when he said, "If you haven't found something worth dying for, you aren't fit to be living."[13]

I sometimes wonder what was going through the disciples' minds in the initial moments of the church. In those first few weeks and months, as a young church, they tried to decipher what their fledgling community was going to look like as they obeyed the commands of Jesus. There must have been times when they were still wondering how it all was going to resolve itself. Their only certainty was that their faith was their only hope.

---

[13] http://www.pitara.com/reference/quotations/quotes-by-source.asp?quotation-source=Dr.+Martin+Luther+King%2C+Jr., (accessed October 29, 2012)

Here is how Luke recounts the events in Acts 4. Peter and John had healed a crippled man who was a beggar at the temple in Jerusalem. He had been there for a long time. This man had little hope for his life to change, but Peter and John offered him the only thing they had to give. They gave him Jesus and the man left there healed. As a result of this healing, Peter and John were charged by the religious leaders for causing a disturbance. As the two apostles faced the charges, everyone present came to the realization that these were not ordinary men. They have been changed because of the one they had encountered and communed with.

> [13] Now when they saw the boldness of Peter and John, and perceived that they were uneducated, common men, they were astonished. And they recognized that they had been with Jesus. ... [18] So they called them and charged them not to speak or teach at all in the name of Jesus. [19] But Peter and John answered them, "Whether it is right in the sight of God to listen to you rather than to God, you must judge, [20] *for we cannot but speak of what we have seen and heard.*" (Acts 4:13, 18-20, emphasis added)

What makes this event so amazing is not that they wiped the sweat from their brows and said to themselves, "Glad we dodged a bullet back there!" No, that is not the response of a man or woman who has seen, heard, and experienced what these disciples had. Peter and John went to their fellowship and they do what under different circumstances would be seen and understood as foolish and careless, possibly even reckless. They ask for boldness to do it again!

This is exactly what they did at their next worship service and prayer meeting. Read this humble request.

> [23] When they were released, they went to their friends and reported what the chief priests and the elders had said to them. … [29] And now, Lord, look upon their threats and *grant to your servants to continue to speak your word with all boldness,* [30] while you stretch out your hand to heal, and signs and wonders are performed through the name of your holy servant Jesus." [31] And when they had prayed, the place in which they were gathered together was shaken, and *they were all filled with the Holy Spirit and continued to speak the word of God with boldness.* (Acts 4:23, 29-31, emphasis added)

Where is this prayer in our churches today? We pray for clarity, openness on the part of the hearer, and even favor with those whom we will encounter. But, why don't we pray for greater boldness? Why do we think that disciples today, twenty centuries removed from the events in the wake of Pentecost, can do better? Why do we pray for things that were not even on the minds of those disciples who were twenty minutes removed from being imprisoned for proclaiming Jesus?

We have been called to faithful and radical obedience. As the Church of Jesus Christ, we must again take a stand and boldly proclaim the truth of the Gospel. We must ask for the boldness to proclaim the Truth of God, which is Jesus himself and by himself.

A Prayer for Boldness

I invite you to pray this prayer if you see in your own life the need for greater boldness.

> O God, help that we who are called by the name of your Son would make boldness a virtue of higher regard than blessing, comfort, or even safety. Boldness is what is needed to minister to the lost and the pretentious alike. Boldness is the antidote to our pride because it forces us to trust in you to guide and deliver us in this life.
>
> I pray for boldness. Grant that I may proclaim Your truth, the message of Jesus the Christ, to a world that prefers to turn a deaf ear to what you have declared in the heavens. The works of your hands are a testimony of your majesty. O that we who are weak would turn to you and trust in your strength and power before those who portend to be powerful and of high repute. There is no name worthy of our total allegiance, but yours.
>
> In the name of the Lion of the tribe of Judah, Jesus the Christ, Amen.

❖ ❖ ❖ ❖ ❖ ❖ ❖ ❖

[1] I mean that the heir, as long as he is a child, is no different from a slave, though he is the owner of everything, [2] but he is under guardians and managers until the date set by his father. [3] In the same way we also, when we were children, were enslaved to the elementary principles of the world. [4] But when the fullness of time had come, God sent forth his Son, born of woman, born under the law, [5] to redeem those who were under the law, so that we might receive adoption as sons. [6] And because you are sons, God has sent the Spirit of his Son into our hearts, crying, "Abba! Father!" [7] So you are no longer a slave, but a son, and if a son, then an heir through God.

Galatians 4:1-7

❖ ❖ ❖ ❖ ❖ ❖ ❖ ❖

Chapter 5

FAITH IS...

CRYING OUT TO THE HEART OF GOD

It was Christmas Eve of 2001. My wife's family and my family were spending some time together over the holiday. This was going to be a special time because my wife (girlfriend at the time) did not know that I was planning on proposing marriage to her that evening. It was both great and terrifying.

I bought the ring months before and had it stashed away where no one would think to look. When I finally made up my mind on what to do, I knew it was going to be a total surprise.

My mom had this small white Scottish poodle toy that had a small envelope stitched to its mouth. It read, "Special delivery just for you." After pinning the ring underneath that envelope, my family and I waited for my future wife and her family to come over to the house. I have to tell you, every time I walked past that dog, I looked at it and knew that as soon as I "popped the question" everything would be different. That our lives would never be the same. I can honestly say that it has not been.

What made that moment even more amazing was that the day before, my sister and my future wife, Miranda, were talking. In the conversation, they come to the topic of marriage and my sister asked Miranda if she even wanted to get married. The irony was that my sister already knew I had the ring and was proposing the next day!

Miranda confided that she wanted to get married but was not sure if I was ever going to get around to it. Little did she know I was going to ask for her hand in marriage the following day. There are many things that make those couple of days memorable, but this story in particular really makes the entire process and event an unforgettable one. This memory reminds me of other situations where there is a desire, an expectation, but there is also a question. Will what we are longing for ever come?

A GREAT GIFT

There are times when the preciousness of a gift cannot be understood until it is longed for. What I mean is that the more we desire something, the greater our joy when we finally get it. This is the sentiment that a child feels during Christmas. The list has been written. The shopping has begun. And so has the anticipation brought on by the wondering of whether or not what has was requested will find its way to the base of the Christmas tree.

Of all the gifts Christ has procured for us through his death, burial, and resurrection, our adoption into the family of God may be one of the greatest and yet poorly articulated of the Christian faith. I am not trying to categorize or prioritize the benefits of our fellowship with God. This is not possible. It would be a fool's errand. What I hope we understand is that each and every gift we receive from God we enjoy all at once. We just can't appreciate them at the same time because our focus may be on only one at any given moment in time.

What I am trying to describe here is that one of the fundamental realities that is now true for us, that was not true before our faith in Christ, is how the very nature of our relationship with God has changed. If we do not recognize this, it becomes increasingly difficult to exercise faith at all. The great truth we are considering in this chapter is that we are no longer enemies of God, deserving of his wrath and punishment. Because of Jesus' sacrifice we are now sons and daughters and heirs with Jesus who can now be disciplined and restored by a loving Father. Let's look at what all of this means.

A SPIRITUAL REALITY

When Paul was teaching the church in Galatia about their new relationship with God, he intentionally used the concept of adoption. Paul was not trying to be sentimental. Adoption was a social and cultural reality his readers would have been familiar with. As modern readers of the Bible we must make sure we do not read into the text a sentimental understanding of what adoption means. I do not mean to diminish adoption in anyway when I say this. I simply want to draw a vital distinction between the modern and ancient conception of adoption. Adoption served an entirely different purpose in the ancient world. It involved far more than our modern practice from both a legal and cultural point of view. In order to understand Paul's usage, we have to keep this difference in view.

Adoption had a greater legal implication for Paul's hearers, which we must understand as well if we are going to make sense of what Paul is teaching.

> Most scholars agree that Paul borrowed the concept of adoption from Greek or Roman law. The Jews did not practice adoption, and the word never appears in the Hebrew scriptures. In *The Epistle to the Romans*, Leon Morris says adoption is "a useful word for Paul, for it signifies being granted the full rights and privileges of [belonging to] a family [in] which one does not belong by nature." One is not born a Christian; one becomes a Christian. This reminds me of my three-year-old friend Grace, who was not born a Roberts, but became a Roberts when her parents adopted her. [14]

---

[14] Verity A. Jones, Cynthia A. Jarvis *Up for Adoption: Romans 8:12-25*, The Christian Century, July 3, 2002 (accessed on

Morris continues, "This is a good illustration of one aspect of Paul's understanding of what it means to become a Christian. The believer is admitted into the heavenly family," a family to which the believer has no rights of his or her own. Not only did the concept of adoption help Paul explain how gentiles and Jews could be part of the same family of God, but it also allowed him to emphasize that salvation is not achieved through a birthright inheritance but because of God's act of grace toward each soul who repents.

"An adopted child is received as a gift by her new family, just as the adopting family is a gift to the child. In the same way, the spirit of adoption that Paul commends to the reader is one of gift. It is Paul's way of describing the gift God gives to us in Christ."[15]

As Paul considered how to best explain what Jesus had been able to do for the person who trusted in him, the apostle found this concept of adoption to be one of the clearest. It is crucial we do not think of this activity as merely some kind of benevolent action on Gods' part. What God did in bringing us into his family was no small miracle (as if there are ever any small miracles), nor was it something that was provided for us with little effort. The implications of what this means **CANNOT** be exaggerated.

---

http://www.religion-online.org/showarticle.asp?title=2653, May 18, 2017) Volume 119, No. 14.

[15] ibid.

At the heart of this expression of faith is the confidence that comes because of what God gives to us, his children. We grow in confidence with our relationship with God because we are given access to God himself. We are not merely spending time with some celestial secretary that makes us wait in line. I'll ask the question this way: how are we to understand what Jesus has secured for us in adoption?

In order to better understand what has happened to us, we have to understand the word Paul used to describe the circumstances of our adoption and the new familial arrangement that was created. The word *huiothesia* is translated "adoption" five times in the New Testament. Each instance is in an epistle written by Paul (Romans 8:15, 23; 9:4; Galatians 4:5; Ephesians 1:5). The *Louw and Nida Lexicon* provides some context for how first century culture understood this term. Adoption was "to formally and legally declare that someone who is not one's own child is henceforth to be treated and cared for as one's own child, including complete rights of inheritance."[16] Paul's apparent intent was to clearly identify the new nature of the relationship created between God and his adopted children because of Jesus' sacrifice on the cross.

God does not make those whom he has adopted into the black sheep of the family. God is the perfect father,

---

[16] Johannes P. Louw and Eugene Albert Nida, vol. 1, *Greek-English Lexicon of the New Testament: Based on Semantic Domains*, electronic ed. of the 2nd edition. (New York: United Bible Societies, 1996), 463-64.

capable of loving all of his children without showing any favoritism. Adoption did not and does not relegate us to a second-class relationship with God in heaven. We have been brought in and have been given the same rights of privilege and inheritance as natural born children. Spiros Zodhiates puts it like this in his dictionary of the New Testament:

> "Paul in these passages is alluding to a Greek and Roman custom rather than a Hebrew one. Since *huiothesía* was a technical term in Roman law for an act that had specific legal and social effects, there is much probability that Paul had some reference to that in his use of the word. Adoption, when thus legally performed, put a man in every respect in the position of a son by birth to him who had adopted him, so that he possessed the same rights and owed the same obligations." [17]

Dr. Timothy George further highlights why Paul's framing of our relationship with God in terms of adoptions is so pivotal. It is not just that we have been given access to God. Our entire standard of living, our complete outlook of the future has been forever altered because of God's gracious love for us.

> Whether the background of Paul's adoption language is Roman or Jewish, it speaks in a powerful way of the

---

[17] Spiros Zodhiates, *The Complete Word Study Dictionary: New Testament*, electronic ed. (Chattanooga, TN: AMG Publishers, 2000).

tremendous transformation in our relationship to God. Through God's gracious initiative we have been delivered out of slavery unto sonship, out of bondage to sin and the powers of destruction produced by it into the glorious liberty of the children of God. [18]

The Bible clearly teaches that adoption is the method God used to bring us into his family. What this means is God has chosen to also give us all of the rights and privileges that belong to Jesus! Not only is this incredible, but it's also nearly incomprehensible.

Our adoption into the family of God is a stunning reality for us to contemplate and examine further. The richness of this concept is sorrowfully lacking in the Church. God's love for us is magnificently displayed in the certificate of adoption signed in the blood of our Savior. When we finally begin to appreciate what it cost God to bring us into the family we must respond in an appropriate way. Worship is the proper response to this extravagant love. We have been born-again into God's family and we can never be cast out again. Our adoption should inspire our faith to cry out to our loving Father with more earnestness than ever before; with every ounce of passion we can muster.

---

[18] Timothy George, vol. 30, *Galatians*, The New American Commentary (Nashville: Broadman & Holman Publishers, 1994), 305-06.

❖ ❖ ❖ ❖ ❖ ❖ ❖ ❖

[5] Have this mind among yourselves, which is yours in Christ Jesus, [6] who, though he was in the form of God, did not count equality with God a thing to be grasped, [7] but made himself nothing, taking the form of a servant, being born in the likeness of men. [8] And being found in human form, he humbled himself by becoming obedient to the point of death, even death on a cross.

Philippians 2:5-8

❖ ❖ ❖ ❖ ❖ ❖ ❖ ❖

Chapter 6

FAITH IS...

CULTIVATING THE MIND OF GOD

I remember hearing a story told of two Moravian missionaries who learned about a colony of slaves.[19] The colony had not yet heard the saving Gospel message of Jesus Christ. As a result, their hearts were burdened for the slaves. So, they sought some opportunity to go and preach to them. However, there did not appear to be any easy solution to the problem of getting to the slaves. The slaves were kept on a remote island, isolated from most of the world. With no solution immediately presenting itself, they prayed for an answer and a plan forward.

---

[19] While finishing the book I discovered that there is some debate surrounding the historicity of this story. However, I have left it included in the text as an aspirational parable of the call of God to every believer to count the cost of God's will in their lives.

These two young missionaries soon discovered that the slave owner had forbidden access to Christian missionaries to the island. One of the slave owner's reasons for keeping the slaves isolated was because he feared the effect the Gospel would have on the productivity of the slaves. After much consideration, the two young men finally came to the realization that the only way to take the Gospel and preach to the slaves was to *sell themselves* into slavery.

That is exactly what they did. They sold themselves into slavery and they bade their families and friends goodbye for the last time. The account records that one of them looked over the rail of the ship, as it pulled from the dock, and screamed to those they would certainly never see again,

"Worthy is the Lamb that was slain to receive the reward of His suffering."

Here is one of the great examples of a mind transformed by the Gospel of Christ. It is a mystery. It boggles the mind to think that anyone would make a decision like this because of what they have heard in the Gospel. When a mind has been changed by the Gospel of Christ, we should not be surprised by what they may feel called to do for the sake of Christ.

This transformation is, I believe, at the heart of what God is seeking and desiring to see in the lives of his children. The hearts and minds of these young, radical missionaries were so changed and conformed to the mission of Christ that selling themselves into slavery did not appear to be extreme, drastic, or unwarranted. As a matter of fact, they ultimately concluded there was no other choice to be made. This was the path laid before them and they chose to go down it with joy.

I think we have forgotten in our modern context there are worse things than death, suffering, or even slavery. The fires of hell and the people who will find themselves there for failing to repent and turn to Jesus are just two reasons to go into the entire world with the Good News!

Worthy *IS* the Lamb!

Only when our sense of calling to obey the demands of the Gospel is higher than our own comfort will we be able to forsake present pleasure for future glory. We have to see that *ALL* this world pretends to offer is not really the world's to give.

WONDER AT AN ALL-KNOWING GOD

One of the ideas the Bible strives to communicate is that the way God operates, and the way God conceives of things is not the same as we do. Now, this may sound like an obvious, "no-brainer" statement and, I will grant that on the surface you would be correct. What I want to point out is that this is not a practical reality for most of us who claim the name of Christian. For most people who willingly identify as followers of Jesus, the way we live our lives tells a significantly different story.

We tend to live as if God agrees with, or at the very least tolerates, how we go about the business of life. Because, hey, we are not perfect, right?! This mindset and general approach to life give us a false sense of security and freedom. However, what we fail to see is this is a mirage. The freedom and security we seek cannot be found substituting our own conceptions of how God operates from what the Scriptures reveal. We have to learn to rely on God's word for God's way of working in the world and in our lives.

What I have realized is the primary reason we should seek to understand how God operates is that God is the only one who knows what true living is. God is life itself. Life can only be found in him. The very scriptures begin with the retelling of events that depend on God's unique ability to give life. And the life he gives is similar to his in kind, and yet fundamentally distinct and unique from God's own. What this means is when the Bible describes humanity as being made in the image of God, there is a "sameness" without there being equality. There is an "otherness" without there being total isolation.

The way God processes information, makes decisions, and understands the world is on a level far beyond anything the human mind can comprehend or even describe. If we do not recognize this difference and adjust our assumptions about what we think we know about how God thinks, if we do not acknowledge our limitedness in trying to understand how God is God, we will fall prey to the greatest human fault—pride. And, in the process, when we fail to make sense of things because we refuse to accept some things are beyond our reach, we will dishonor God for not letting us in on his plans. We will call into question God's character and will blame God for our finitude. While all this is going on we will have gotten in our own way and will not be able to receive what God is attempting to give—his grace, peace, and love.

The Bible is filled with promises and blessings and curses, and God's perspective is not limited by time, space, or consciousness. God comprehends all things perfectly. (Even thinking about what this means makes my brain hurt.) He sees everything as it should be and works to make it so when it is not that way. Therefore, faith's task in the life of the believer is to move closer and closer toward the way God thinks, to conform our lives to his patterns.

When our thinking is brought into alignment with God's, we will be able to apprehend much more of what God is doing, even when we cannot comprehend all that he is doing. The difference between these two points is the difference of knowing my car works when I put my key in the ignition and understanding *how* it works.

The mystery here is that there is a way of knowing that does not necessarily mean knowing everything in detail. We have to refrain from wanting to have complete knowledge and move toward a full and intimate relationship with God based on the information we have available. A relationship that is both rational and intuitive.

Now, there are some who would see this as settling for less, in which case it would be a misunderstanding of what I mean. In John's Gospel, there is an interesting phrase in the twentieth chapter that may help clarify what I have in mind. In John 20:30-31 we find this postscript:

> [30] Now Jesus did many other signs in the presence of the disciples, *which are not written* in this book; [31] but *these are written* so that you may believe that Jesus is the Christ, the Son of God, and that by believing you may have life in his name. (Emphasis added.)

The reason I find these two verses significant is that in the very pages of the Scriptures we are told, not everything that Jesus did was recorded! However, what was recorded is enough for us to know who Jesus is and what we can expect from receiving and accepting this information. What this means for us is we don't need to know everything; we only need to know the right things. And, when we remember those things, we can have confidence in what we believe. Our goal should be to make sure that we are looking in the right places and trusting in the correct information so we can live in the right way.

THE MIND OF JESUS

The passage in Philippians 2 at the start of the chapter is interesting for several reasons. The primary reason is that it demonstrates the practical application of what it means to live a life that has cultivated the mind of God. Jesus is our ultimate and final example for everything in life. He is the one who best demonstrated and actualized a God-centered way of thinking. When we do not push ourselves to surrender our own ideas and philosophies to God's, we are intentionally moving away from him.

Making the cultivation of the mind of God the central work of our faith development will put us in a truer trajectory to perceiving God's direction in our lives. It will also give us confidence in determining God's instructions in our lives. One of the greatest fears among the people of God is the struggle of knowing the will of God. How are we going to figure out what God wants from us and for us?

If I strive to develop the mindset of faith I will become more pliable to the Spirit's leading in my life. Spending time in prayer, meditation on scripture, acts of service, evangelism, the reading of scripture, and a multitude of other spiritual disciplines will put us in proximity to those ordinary means of grace[20] that God has given to us as his

---

[20] I use the phrase "means of grace" to describe the ways God is able to show us his grace. It could be as simple as a kind word given or a generous deed performed toward us. I call these ordinary because they should be expected. When we are living a *normal* Christian life, then our conduct becomes a vehicle in which God can show his love and grace to those in our circle of influence.

children. These practices will provide us with opportunities to focus our attention on what God is doing and attempting to do in, through, and around us.

Paul in his letter to the Romans provides us with something that approaches a kind of "cause and effect" definition to this reality, without being one exactly. Read carefully what he identifies as the enemy of cultivating the mind of God in our lives.

> 2 Do not be conformed to this world, but be transformed by the renewal of your mind, that by testing you may discern what is the will of God, what is good and acceptable and perfect. (Romans 12:2)

Did you see it? Paul warns the Romans, reminding them they were either going to be conformed to the world's way of thinking or have a transformed mind that reflects Jesus' life. There is no third option. Jesus must be set as the only alternative to everything else. The implication of thinking like this is to demarcate a clear line in the marketplace of religious ideas. Jesus is the only and best option available. That is why learning Jesus' way of thinking and following his example in every facet of life is the only way of ensuring we are moving in the right direction.

THE PROMISE OF A RENEWED MIND

In the pursuit of a renewed mind, what we are striving to achieve is the ability to discern the will of God.

The great fear of the faithful is answered in the struggle to conform every thought and desire to the patterns of the mind of God. Consider for a moment what this means. The longer and more intentionally we cultivate the mind of God, the greater our chances of actually knowing the will of God. Now, that is not something to be overlooked or minimized or categorized as an overstatement. The implication of Paul's instructions is that increased awareness and renewed thinking will only come when the patterns of thought emanating from the world are replaced with those proceeding from God. We cannot continue to think as the world thinks and expect God to work in our lives.

One of the critical changes that occurs as our minds are renewed, and I would argue **MUST** occur, is the way a Christian thinks must change. To fail in this would be to seek out salvation and sanctification on our terms rather than God's. There is a non-negotiable requirement to have faith in and be a follower of Christ. We are not here to continue thinking with the patterns and categories of the world. We must become increasingly like our Savior, having the same mind Jesus had as he fulfilled God's will. The mind of God does not come by accident. It must be cultivated intentionally each and every day.

❖❖❖❖❖❖❖❖

"24 Now I rejoice in my sufferings for your sake, and in my flesh I am filling up what is lacking in Christ's afflictions for the sake of his body, that is, the church, 25 of which I became a minister according to the stewardship from God that was given to me for you, to make the word of God fully known, 26 the mystery hidden for ages and generations but now revealed to his saints. 27 To them God chose to make known how great among the Gentiles are the riches of the glory of this mystery, which is Christ in you, the hope of glory. 28 Him we proclaim, warning everyone and teaching everyone with all wisdom, that we may present everyone mature in Christ. 29 For this I toil, struggling with all his energy that he powerfully works within me.

Colossians 1:24-29

❖❖❖❖❖❖❖❖

Chapter 7

FAITH IS...

Consummating the Mission of God

Of all the choices I have made in my life, there is really only one choice I regret. The reason I regret it is because I made it twice!

My dad, an active duty Army chaplain at the time, had just been stationed in Augusta, Georgia. It was the middle of my tenth-grade year of high school and baseball season was beginning a couple of weeks after we arrived. I decided I would try out for the team. Well, I did not know that the first thing you had to do was run three miles under a certain amount of time. When I found this out, I freaked out. I told my dad I was not going to be able to do it, so I was not even going to go out for the team. He talked me into going for the first day and to see how it went. It was a horrible experience. I almost sprained my ankle; I vomited at least once (that I can remember) and felt like I was going to die. After the first day, I quit.

The following year, I worked up the nerve to try out again. I really did not prepare myself, even though I knew what was coming. I went out the first day and almost made my time. But, when I got home I told my dad what happened. I told him that it was not worth the effort, and I quit again. For two years in a row, I made the same decision. I did not have a good reason. I was lazy and did not want to put in the effort. I wanted all the accolades that came with being a baseball player but was not willing to do what it took to get there. As a result of these two choices, I became a quitter. After that, I began to see myself as a quitter.

Those two decisions shaped my identity for the next fifteen years of my life. I found it easier to quit, hide out, be lazy, and walk away. What I did not realize at the time was how these decisions had shaped my perception of myself. When we leave unfinished business in our lives, we establish patterns that are oftentimes difficult to recognize and change. It took a long time for me to understand why I tended toward quitting rather than following through.

Every day I struggle. I struggle to not give in when a situation requires me to persevere; to not walk away when I need to stand my ground; to not be lazy when I need to be diligent. I am a recovering quitter. This is who I became, but it is not who God made me to be. I became someone other than who God wanted because I had not discovered the power of finishing what I started. I have had to learn what it means to persevere in the midst of my own insecurities because when I do not, I am the one who suffers.

THE MISSION OF GOD

What does it mean to consummate? Webster's dictionary defines consummate in this way: "To finish, complete, make perfect or achieve." So, the question that we have to ask ourselves is this: In what way, or in what sense, does God's mission need to be completed? What is lacking? And more importantly, when we talk about something being missing in what God sent Jesus to do are we verging on the heretical? Or, is there something we do not yet fully understand?

It may be helpful to take a moment and identify what we mean by "the mission of God." If we are supposed to complete it, it would be helpful to understand what God is doing. Paul made this remarkable connection for the believers in Corinth, which I believe is useful for us today. Paul tied together what God was doing in heaven and what Jesus initiated on earth. This joint venture was completed and yet unfulfilled. Let's look at how Paul said it in 2 Corinthians 5:17-21.

> [17] Therefore, if anyone is in Christ, he is a new creation. The old has passed away; behold, the new has come. [18] All this is from God, who through Christ reconciled us to himself and gave us the ministry of reconciliation; [19] that is, *in Christ God was reconciling*

the world to himself, not counting their trespasses against them, and entrusting to us the message of reconciliation. [20] Therefore, we are ambassadors for Christ, God making his appeal through us. We implore you on behalf of Christ, be reconciled to God. [21] For our sake he made him to be sin who knew no sin, so that in him we might become the righteousness of God. (emphasis added)

The spreading of the "message of reconciliation" is the mission God had in mind from eternity past and will ensure is accomplished until the end of time and into eternity future. In Jesus, God was reconciling the world back to himself. God was restoring the order of the world after the chaos of sin had been unleashed. The power of God's grace to put back together again a universe shattered by sin reflects God's power, mercy, and longsuffering kindness.

In order to know our place in God's plan, we have to have a firm grasp of God's heart. When all is said and done, God's grace affords wretched sinners access to himself. The love of God for this fallen world cannot be adequately described because human words have not been invented that could describe God's essential being. Who God is in totality is truly beyond superlatives.

COMPLETING THE COMPLETE

Paul was very deliberate in choosing how he described his ministry to the Colossians. Paul was an educated man and he understood that words have meaning and the wrong word would convey the wrong meaning. As contemporary readers, we have to consider very carefully what Paul said in Colossians 1. If we are not careful we may inadvertently assume something that is not true or, even worse, blasphemous. What exactly did Paul want the believers in Colossi to understand and participate in with him?

If we take a moment and consider the timeline of events up to this point in Paul's ministry we may make some helpful connections. God sent Jesus into the world, in human form, as a baby. Jesus lived upon the earth, ministered, and ultimately was murdered for what he was and what he did. After three days in the grave, Jesus was resurrected, spends the next fifty days verifying his resurrection and then is gone from the earth. These are the events that took place, spelled out in broad strokes.

It may not be apparent right away, but there is a problem in extending the mission beyond the life of the first disciples. It is here where we begin to see a problem in God's plan of reconciling the world back to himself. If Jesus is no longer physically present on earth, how is the Gospel going to be proclaimed to all the people who have not yet heard it? The answer lies in this interesting truth: Jesus is the head of the church. And the church is his body! We are the ones who have been left and specifically tasked with the responsibility to take the message we have heard and received to those who have not.

The mistake some believers make when they read that something is "lacking in Christ's afflictions" is the false conclusion that God is limited in some way. That somehow God made a mistake or failed to calculate the odds for the cost of redemption. This could not be further from the truth. God was fully cognizant of what he was doing. Therefore, we have to take a different view of what Paul is saying here.

GOD INVITES YOU INTO HIS PLAN

So, what is "lacking in Christ's afflictions?" Nothing is lacking from the standpoint of God's part in the plan of salvation. However, everything is lacking from the perspective of the hearers. Jesus, from the beginning, was preparing the disciples to be the heralds who would go into the world with the news of salvation. Jesus knew there was going to be no greater witness to the transforming power of the Gospel than the lives of those who had been changed by the very Gospel they proclaimed.

If Paul had not become an active and intentional participant in the mission of God, the Gospel would not have been spread as quickly. This is why, as followers of Christ, we must see our faith not merely as an internal and personal activity. Our participation in the mission of God has global as well as eternal consequences. And, our involvement has been a part of God's plan from the beginning. This may be the one aspect of the Church's mission that has been misunderstood and inadequately taught over the centuries. We are what is lacking!

If the mission of God is going to be completed we, the Church, must become the agents who see that what is missing, or lacking, in Christ's afflictions is our commitment to step up in boldness and step out in faith. The truth of the matter is God has invited us to be participants in his plan. And the reason we are encouraged to be a part of it at all is so we can see and enjoy the glorious miracle of souls being saved.

The mystery to me has always been why God would invite fallen sinners to participate in the mission? The answer is this: The reason that makes the most sense is that as our loving Father, he desires for us to enjoy his work. God desires that we have some ownership in the work he is doing and thereby can experience joy as we see God at work in the marvel of saving sinners. Therefore, as we participate and enjoy his work in and through us we are some of the first to arrive "on the scene" to see everything God has been able to accomplish through us.

In conclusion, let me clarify what this does not mean. It does not mean God **NEEDS** us to fulfill and accomplish his mission. That would make us the *central* element of God's plan. God does not need our presence or abilities. What God needs are witnesses. And, because we are witnesses to God's saving power and grace, God remains at the center of the story, right where he belongs. Our participation in consummating the mission of God is a gift. And it is one we should not squander.

❖ ❖ ❖ ❖ ❖ ❖ ❖ ❖

[10] For a day in your courts is better
than a thousand elsewhere.

I would rather be a doorkeeper in the house of my
God than dwell in the tents of wickedness.

[11] For the LORD God is a sun and shield;
the LORD bestows favor and honor.

No good thing does he withhold
from those who walk uprightly.

[12] O LORD of hosts,
blessed is the one who trusts in you!

Psalm 84:10-11

❖ ❖ ❖ ❖ ❖ ❖ ❖ ❖

Chapter 8

FAITH IS...

YEARNING FOR THE PRESENCE OF GOD

There are many exciting events and situations in the Bible. There are circumstances of heroism, cowardice, intrigue, and mystery. There are mundane facts and astonishing revelations. We see the heights and the depths of humanity. Both fervent faith and abject depravity are woven throughout the narrative of the Scriptures. And, in the midst of all of these, there is one moment that captures and highlights what it means to desire to be together with God. Of all the recollections in the Bible, the exchange between Moses and God on Mount Sinai is one of the more provocative. When we understand what Moses requested of God, we are forced to consider our own sentiments toward God and his promises.

If you don't remember the story allow me to share with you what happened. Moses had seen some amazing things: the ten plagues in Egypt, the parting of the Red Sea, the destruction of the Egyptian army, and the giving of the Ten Commandments. But, there was something missing. Even though God had been at work in Moses' life, even though Moses had been a witness to some of the most remarkable and unimaginable events the Bible records, a longing remained in Moses' heart.

In Exodus 33 we find an unusual exchange between Moses and God. Moses was not satisfied and he was actually getting to the point of desperation. God had been good. God had provided and protected the people of Israel. However, for Moses, the corporate promises did not remove the longing in his heart to be personally and intimately connected with God. So, Moses asked God to do something dangerous. Moses asked to see God's face. What is dangerous about this you ask? Read God's own words of caution to get a sense of the seriousness of what Moses was asking.

> [20] "[You] cannot see my face, for man shall not see me and live." (Exodus 33:20)

Moses had reached a point in his life where he was willing to die so he could be with God. It was not just frustration with the people he was leading either. To see this request in this light would be terribly shortsighted. There was something more significant at work in Moses' heart; something that could only be satisfied with a personal and intimate encounter with God.

We can say this about the nature of the request because Moses did not ask to be in God's presence. That would have pointed to Moses' displeasure with his current location. The specificity of the request is revealing. Moses wanted to see God's face. This is an ancient description of relationship, of an intimate closeness to the one to whom you make the request.

Are we like that? Many of us would like to think we are getting close to this kind of yearning. Others of us know we are nowhere near. Maybe a better question would be, "Do we want to be like that?" Do we want to be in the presence of God more than we want anything else, more than our very lives?

A BELIEVER'S GREATEST DESIRE

If someone were to ask me what should be the greatest desire for every follower of Jesus I would articulate it in the following way:

Believers in Jesus yearn to be in the presence of God more than anything else.

For some, this may be a bit much to take in or even accept as viable. How could this or, better yet, why should this be the "greatest" desire we hold as believers? This is an honest and important question. Not one that can be set aside quickly or dismissed out of hand. Before we continue, think about how you would answer? What is your greatest desire? What is it you yearn for more than anything else? How is that driving and motivating your thoughts and actions right now?

As I have thought about what faith is, I do not see how we can avoid this question. What is it that we should want for ourselves? Should it not be what God, our heavenly Father, desires for us? Should it not be to have and enjoy, right now, the eternal fellowship he has promised for all his children? The way we think about what this means for us will depend, in large part, on how we understand who God is and our relationship with him.

I will admit this sounds foreign to modern ears. This is not our typical way of thinking and we may find it hard to believe how anything other than our lives here on earth could be better. I understand this. I really do. We do not have anybody else's report of what happens when we die, so it becomes easier to focus our attention on the life we have now. We know what to expect even when it is difficult. We know the tendencies and patterns of those whom we love and those whom we would rather not know. There is a certain predictability to the unpredictable nature of life on this planet. So, many of us, the followers of Jesus, tend to choose what we know, as flawed and imperfect as it may be, for what we do not yet know.

The problem with growing more satisfied with what we have now is it does not maintain the proper value of the sacrifice of Christ in view. In a way, we cheapen what Jesus provided through his death and resurrection because we simply do not know how to agree with the Bible's testimony of our future hope.

I am not saying we are supposed to know what to expect on the other side of death. Or even what the process of dying will be like or feel like. What I am saying is that we are not as hopeful for what is to come as we should be because, in the back of our minds, we do not know if we can trust the one who promised to prepare the way. Or whether what he said about what awaits us is even true! I know that seems drastic but is there really another explanation for our anemic longing to be in God's presence?

Listen to Jesus' words to his disciples:

> [1] "Do not let your hearts be troubled. You believe in God; believe also in me. [2] My Father's house has many rooms; if that were not so, would I have told you that I am going there to prepare a place for you? [3] *And if I go and prepare a place for you, I will come back and take you to be with me that you also may be where I am.* [4] You know the way to the place where I am going."... [6] Jesus answered, "I am the way and the truth and the life. No one comes to the Father except through me. (John 14:1-4, 6, emphasis added)

The reason we should trade what we know for what we do not know is because that is what the Bible says we should do. I know that may not satisfy many of us. However, we cannot pick and choose what we take on faith and what we try and second-guess. In the same way, salvation is received as an act of faith, so is the promise of our future hope. If we can rest in the comfort of what God has done in Jesus, we should accept the promise Jesus has outlined about our future existence.

I think what we often fail to realize is that the trade is not from something higher, this life, for something of less value, life with God. (Even writing that last sentence reveals the flawed thinking that has seeped into the Church about our future hope.) What this world has to offer is not only flawed, broken, and deteriorating; what this world offers is contrary to anything and everything God has prepared for us. As a matter of fact, the higher our attachment to this world and the things in it (including our loved ones!) the greater our distance from and the smaller our love for God! The apostle John tells us as much in 1 John 2:15-17, where he says that loving the world and the things in it means we do not have the love of the Father in us at all!

> ¹⁵ Do not love the world or the things in the world. *If anyone loves the world, the love of the Father is not in him.* ¹⁶ For all that is in the world—the desires of the flesh and the desires of the eyes and pride of life—is not from the Father but is from the world. ¹⁷ And the world is passing away along with its desires, but

whoever does the will of God abides forever. (Emphasis added)

John's words are so stark, it sobers the mind. Is it any wonder this passage of scripture is not often preached? Take a couple of minutes and read that passage again. This passage is one of the most unequivocal declarations in the Bible of the divide that exists between the world and God. Our loyalties must be definitively spelled out. Not for God's sake but for our own.

WHAT I SEE IS NOT WHAT I GET

Our understanding of and longing for what is to come reveals, in no small measure, the level of our trust in God. When our desire is for a continued life here in this world, the call of heaven has been muted. The belongings and possessions we attach our hearts to can help us determine where our focus is directed.

I want to clarify something here. I do not want to give the impression that our relationships with our family and friends are to be minimized or dismissed out of hand, or that we have to sell all the stuff we have. That is not what I am getting after. What I am asking is for us to consider if we have allowed anything, including our relationships and our things, to get between us and God. I love my wife and my children. I would do anything for them. I would give my life for them. What gives me pause is this: *Why then will I not do the same thing for God, who has saved my soul from eternal suffering and separation from him by sending Jesus?*

If Jesus is the embodiment of God on earth (and he is!), then accepting this reality must have practical and visible effects in how we live. On this point, Paul's life serves as an excellent example of what a life conformed to the reality of Christ's life on earth is supposed to look like. Paul's transformation was something that did not happen overnight. In fact, it was a process that took more than a decade to fully work its way out in Paul's life.[21] Only someone who truly possesses the mind of Christ and who has been conformed into the image of Jesus would say the things Paul said and mean them. An example of this is found in Romans 8.

> [18] For I consider that the sufferings of this present time are not worth comparing with the glory that is to be revealed to us. [19] For the creation waits with eager longing for the revealing of the sons of God. [20] For the creation was subjected to futility, not willingly, but because of him who subjected it, in hope [21] that the creation itself will be set free from its bondage to corruption and obtain the freedom of the glory of the children of God. [22] For we know that the whole creation has been groaning together in the pains of childbirth until now. [23] And not only the creation, but

---

[21] While it is difficult to determine how much time passed between Paul's conversion and his first official missionary journey, most sources point to a time of no less than ten years and no more than fourteen years.

we ourselves, who have the firstfruits of the Spirit, groan inwardly as we wait eagerly for adoption as sons, the redemption of our bodies. 24 For in this hope we were saved. Now hope that is seen is not hope. For who hopes for what he sees? 25 But if we hope for what we do not see, we wait for it with patience. (Romans 8:18-25)

That last verse is just crazy… on the surface. Paul is essentially saying that if we are hoping in what we have seen we are **NOT** truly hoping at all. Paul is calling us to a deeper understanding and expression of Christian hope. If we stop and evaluate what Paul is challenging us to consider, we will have to ask ourselves, "What is the true value of what Jesus has done for us?" Better yet, how do "I" feel about Jesus dying for "my" sin on the cross? Paul is challenging us to consider how the most authentic expression of hope is found in longing for what we do not yet have. It is the promise of future hope that is of greater value and worth than anything and everything in this world.

To put this idea into a practical example, we can look at the work of evangelism. When we share the Gospel, we are asking people to accept a past event as the key that unlocks a future reality. The problem most people have to face and overcome is the distance between the work of salvation by Jesus on the cross and the time a sinner hears and believes. This affects a person's willingness and ability to become committed, life-long disciples. In other words, the personalization of the Gospel will always be the great challenge of evangelism. Until a soul feels the weight of the glory of God's grace within it, the Gospel will not filter into the depths of who they are. Paul seems to be describing the internalization of the Gospel as the beginning of the hope we do not yet see.

When we are able to internalize Christ's sacrifice, we begin to approach what Paul is pointing to. Paul said that going through suffering is worth whatever it costs *precisely* because of the glory of Christ and his work within us. When we contemplate on what Paul endured, we begin to get a sense of how much more valuable Paul understood Jesus to be compared to everything else around him. Look at another example from Paul's letter to the Roman church.

> [16] So we do not lose heart. Though our outer self is wasting away, our inner self is being renewed day by day. [17] *For this light momentary affliction is preparing for us an eternal weight of glory beyond all comparison,* [18] as we look not to the things that are seen but to the things that are unseen. For the things that are seen are transient, but the things that are unseen are eternal. (Romans 4:16-18)

Again, Paul outlines the parameters and the issues. What we are experiencing now are "light and momentary afflictions." Our heavenly imagination must expand so we can see what is to come as more valuable, and ultimately, more desirable than what we have in "the here and now." What is to come is "beyond all comparison,"

Paul says. The present realities are not as real as we think them to be. No, they are transient; they are passing away. Not because they are bad but because we will not endure forever in this form. We will be changed, transformed into what the Lord intended and designed before sin destroyed, diminished, and defaced God's good creation.

WE ARE NOT HOME YET

We are strangers here. That is the bottom line. We do not belong on this cursed earth, living under the burden of sin. We were destined to be in God's presence before the fall of humanity and we who trust in Christ are now destined for a new city in a renewed world. This is the reality Abraham and all who believe as he did are hanging on to, with faith. Our hope is not tied to God's ability to restrain sin, as thankful as we are for this. Our hope and joy are bound together in God's promise to re-create all that is and put it into the state he desired it to be when he spoke the first creative word.

The writer of Hebrews captures the essence of what it means to yearn after the presence of God far better than I can. After reminding the readers of the many who walked in faith, a turn takes place and the writer offers an explanation for why these early believers hoped and believed.

> [13] These all died in faith, not having received the things promised, but having seen them and greeted them from afar, and having acknowledged that they

were strangers and exiles on the earth. [14] For people who speak thus make it clear that they are seeking a homeland. [15] If they had been thinking of that land from which they had gone out, they would have had opportunity to return. [16] But as it is, *they desire a better country*, that is, a heavenly one. Therefore God is not ashamed to be called their God, for he has prepared for them a city. (Hebrews 11:13-16, emphasis added)

Faith is a yearning for the promised communion that comes from being in the presence of our God and heavenly Father. The question we must face and decisively answer is this: Do we desire the better country, the heavenly country God is calling us to? Or, are we satisfied here?

My prayer is that my heart would yearn for the presence of God above all else.

❖ ❖ ❖ ❖ ❖ ❖ ❖ ❖

³⁹ And he came out and went, as was his custom, to the Mount of Olives, and the disciples followed him. ⁴⁰ And when he came to the place, he said to them, "Pray that you may not enter into temptation." ⁴¹ And he withdrew from them about a stone's throw, and knelt down and prayed, ⁴² saying, "Father, if you are willing, remove this cup from me. Nevertheless, not my will, but yours, be done." ⁴³ And there appeared to him an angel from heaven, strengthening him. ⁴⁴ And being in an agony he prayed more earnestly; and his sweat became like great drops of blood falling down to the ground. ⁴⁵ And when he rose from prayer, he came to the disciples and found them sleeping for sorrow, ⁴⁶ and he said to them, "Why are you sleeping? Rise and pray that you may not enter into temptation."

Luke 22:39-46

❖ ❖ ❖ ❖ ❖ ❖ ❖ ❖

Chapter 9

FAITH IS...

SURRENDERING TO THE WILL OF GOD

I remember the night Jesus changed the trajectory of my life forever. It was September 21, 1997. On this pivotal Sunday night, God called me into full-time ministry by giving me the courage to walk with him rather than on my own path.

I was sitting in the back of the church my family was attending. I had gone alone because I had been wandering away from God and what I knew about his word. My parents and I were not seeing eye-to-eye at the time, but I knew they would let me go to church. So, I went, more to escape my house than anything else. If you have ever been angry at God, going to his house may not be the best idea.

I sat there in one of the darker corners of the church during that evening service, minding my own business, when I began to listen to the pastor and what he was saying. He was relating the story in Luke 22, the story of Jesus praying in the garden of Gethsemane. But, it was the question he asked that really grabbed my heart: **Why did Jesus endure all that he suffered?** Something about the question captured my attention and pricked at my heart. The longer I sat there, the more I thought about the situation the question pointed to. And, the more I thought about the issue, the more I felt the realization washing over me. I did not have an answer and could not come up with one that made any sense.

My mind started to race and my heart was beating harder and harder in my chest. The longer I sat there in that dark corner of the room, the heavier the weight I was feeling seemed to get. I could not explain what was happening nor could I have anticipated what was about to happen.

The pastor then proceeded to describe the sham of a trial, the lies that were told by false witnesses, and even the cross and the death that was to come. As he talked, he pointed in my direction (you know, one of those "unintentional" preacher gestures to some random place in the building). As he pointed, he said something like this.

> "The reason that Jesus endured the garden and the cross and the tomb was because he looked past all of that and He saw YOU!"

I will never forget those last three words. They are seared in my memory for all time. When he finished that statement, with his finger pointed, seemingly through my chest, I felt a weight lift from my shoulders and my heart. I cannot explain it, but I began to cry as the full weight of what that reality meant for me as an individual. For the first time, I came to understand what Jesus had done so that I might have true life. I prayed that night that if God could help me right what had been going wrong in my life, I would do whatever he asked me to do. It has not always been easy since that night, but I have never turned back from my promise.

SALVATION IS NOT SELFISH

One of the most challenging realities of the Christian journey is this: *It's not about me.* Jesus did not die so I could have everything I ever wanted. God did not orchestrate the greatest rescue mission in the history of the cosmos so we could gather around dinner tables and reminisce about how bad it was "out there" before we were rescued. This kind of thinking flies in the face of what the Bible teaches and, more importantly, it diminishes the worth and glory of God himself. Any and every failure on our part to live our lives according to the sacrifice of Christ is a travesty and an insult to God's grace and love.

Ok, I know all of that was a mouthful, but let's take some time and think about it. God did not send his Son on a mission of redemption, and Jesus did not die for the sins of the world so that we could continue living our lives focused on our own desires. Selfishness should never be the resulting effect of a sacrifice of that magnitude.

If we can so quickly forget where we were, where we were heading and move on from the fact that hell was our final destination, something is very wrong. But, maybe, that is precisely the issue. We don't fully understand the gravity of the situation Jesus rescued us from. Perhaps, we don't want to think about the fact that our sin is as awful and disgusting as God says it is. I believe our failure to recognize how bad our situation was and is without God is fundamentally the matter that must be resolved by every person who claims to be a follower of Jesus.

I look at this event in the garden during Jesus' ministry and I am reminded of what it took for me to be saved; what it took for me to enjoy the pleasure of God's company forever; what it took for me to no longer fear death and the grave and the torment of hell. Jesus had to suffer so that I would not have to.

GOD SUFFERS BECAUSE OF SIN

Jesus pleaded with God the Father in prayer. He moved away from his disciples, maybe for privacy, maybe Jesus didn't want the disciples hearing him pleading with God to get out of this situation, I do not know. What I do know is that Jesus called out to God and was in need of comfort and reassurance. Even Jesus, whose existence was also defined by his full humanity, felt the pressing weight of what was about to happen to him. Any person who thinks that God takes pleasure is sending people to hell must turn to this moment and remember this truth: *In Jesus, the Triune God experienced the torment of a potential eternity in hell!*

On the cross, the full wrath of God for the entire history of sin was laid upon the shoulders of Jesus and in that moment, God understood what was to come for every soul that perishes separated from him. Some might think that this is taking it too far. No, the mystery of the Trinity does not need to be explained for the reality that Jesus experienced separation from God to be seen. If Jesus is God the Son (and he is), then we have to see, that at Calvary, the three persons of the Trinity had the perfect fellowship that defines the nature of God broken because of sin. Sin does not only affect humanity. Sin entered into and affected the experience of God's very own existence. And God chose to let it! Let that sink in for a moment.

From start to finish, salvation was God's idea. There is nothing we can do to change God's mind. That is why when the Bible says that "where sin increased, grace abounded all the more" (Romans 5:20) it is so amazing. Even though the cost of sin is great and even though the penalty of sin is horrible, God's grace and love and mercy reach out from heaven and somehow unravel the tangled mess of our lives. Herein is the miracle of salvation. Here is where the wonder of grace is found. This is what it means to be loved unconditionally by a holy and compassionate God.

HOW FAR ARE YOU WILLING TO GO?

This moment in Jesus' journey on earth reveals a couple of important realities. First, *Jesus is our model for everything pertaining to the faith*. In everything that Jesus said and did we are confronted and challenged to evaluate where we stand. When we think about what God has called us to, how often do we see it as a challenge? Do we understand that it may be difficult to accomplish the task that is set before us? However, even in the midst of the difficulties, Jesus stands as our exemplar for living.

Too often we think that by giving up an hour or two a week, or even a weekend once a year, that that somehow qualifies as a sacrifice. This is more of an inconvenience than a sacrifice. "It is what I did when I could squeeze it in." Some of you who will read this will probably think this is unfair, overstated, or just plain ridiculous. And you would be wrong. Jesus himself said we should not be surprised that the world hates us (Matthew 10:22, John 15:10). But, most of us are not hated by the world. Jesus said that if we are going to follow after him that we should take up our cross every day (Luke 9:23). What do you think a cross is for? We are not taking up Jesus' cross. We are supposed to take up our own cross and then follow him to our own Calvary, our own place of death. But, nobody wants a Christianity that demands that much. We want our appointments with Jesus to be fun, care free, encouraging, and uplifting. None of us wants a hard faith, a demanding master, a difficult journey, or a sorrow-filled life. If that was what the church was selling, we might just see smaller churches overall and churches shrinking in membership than what we already have.

But the second reality that stands out here is this: *The will of God is worth the cost.* Many of us are familiar with the phrase Jesus uses here, "Not my will, by yours be done." Many of us may even have used that phrase. But, notice that in this simple phrase Jesus is declaring God's will as more important and worthy of everything it costs to see it done. It does not matter what it takes, God's will be done!

I am growing in my conviction that a life spent doing the will of God will not be a wasted or misspent life. Even so, I get the sense from time to time that this is exactly what some Christians have come to believe. To give God everything and to forsake our own desires would in some way be unfair to us. Was it fair for Jesus to die for sins he did not commit? Was it fair for Jesus to be humiliated because no one had the courage to speak up and tell the truth? Is it fair that I continue to live my life according to my own desires and do not really stop to consider what God would want?

Faith in Christ is not about things being fair. Faith in Christ is about recognizing what has been done for us and what needs to be done by us. On both counts, God is the one who chooses what that means. The time has come for each of us to deal with the ramifications of disobedience. In the end, we must either accept or reject the idea that faith is surrendering to the will of God in all things and at all times.

❖ ❖ ❖ ❖ ❖ ❖ ❖ ❖

[1] Now the serpent was more crafty than any other beast of the field that the Lord God had made. He said to the woman, "Did God actually say,"… [8] And they heard the sound of the Lord God walking in the garden in the cool of the day, and the man and his wife hid themselves from the presence of the Lord God among the trees of the garden. [9] But the Lord God called to the man and said to him, "Where are you?" [10] And he said, "I heard the sound of you in the garden, and I was afraid, because I was naked, and I hid myself." [11] He said, "Who told you that you were naked? Have you eaten of the tree of which I commanded you not to eat?"

Genesis 3:1a, 8-11

❖ ❖ ❖ ❖ ❖ ❖ ❖ ❖

Chapter 10

FAITH IS...

SATISFIED WITH THE PERSON OF GOD

I was sitting in my chair in the living room listening to something on my computer when I looked up and noticed my one-year-old daughter, Addie, looking at me. She was playing with one of the many toys littering the living room floor. I wasn't anticipating what was about to happen. It happened so quickly, but it left an indelible mark on me.

I'm not sure I can explain what happened in that little exchange of glances. She looked at me with her toothy grin and I realized, in a way I had never experienced before, what it meant to be accepted for who I was. We have all heard about those moments before. And many of us are fortunate enough to experience one or two of them in our lives. I can honestly say this was one of the few moments in my life where I recall the exact moment and it came from a source I did not anticipate.

This is what I mean. My daughter knows no other daddy. I am the only one she has and will ever have. In spite of my many flaws and imperfections, at least in her eyes, in that moment I was perfect. She does not always understand what I say or do. And yet, she is (mostly) satisfied with me. She had not gotten old enough to be disappointed in me for what I do, what I have (or do not have), or what I might have said. In that split second, I knew I was loved just the way I am.

God has an eternal capacity to love us as his creation and as his children. There is nothing that will change God's desire to extend grace and demonstrate love to us. The challenge on this journey of faith is avoiding any attempt to reinterpret what God has said about his own character and intentions. When we start down this road we cut our faith loose from the moorings of God's word, the only source of truth available to us for salvation.

To understand our tendency to re-write our own faith history we will look at how our relationship with God was changed. We need to understand the nature of sin and the effect it has had on the Divine-human relationship. The better we understand our relationship with God the more apparent the path will be toward consistently practicing our faith.

SIN LEADS TO BROKEN FELLOWSHIP

Let's start our conversation about sin with an easy question. What was the first sin? Okay, maybe not so simple. The retelling of sin's entrance into the world is recorded in the third chapter of Genesis. It has been described in different ways: pride, greed, ignorance, and being deceived by the devil. In the end, it does not matter what you call the first sin, there is one undeniable certainty that remains. At the root of the first sin was a failure to be satisfied with God and God alone. Adam and Eve's sin led to a broken relationship with God because they were deceived into believing there was something "better" out there.

As we continue to look at what faith is, we will now take time to consider that faith must be pointed at something. A faith that is not moving, or said another way, a faith that does not cause us to move toward God, is not faith in any biblical sense. Faith, fundamentally, is an action word. Faith must describe what is being done by the person who claims to have it. The only characteristics that gives the word faith its particular and unique meaning is when we talk about it in a Christian sense. Any other understanding of faith makes faith an affirmation of systems and philosophies.

When we are talking about faith in the Christian sense, we are doing so in connection to the object our faith is pointed to. Faith is not a place or state of being. The object of our faith is actually a person whom we seek to be in relationship with. No other religion conceives of faith in this way. As followers of Jesus and believers in the Gospel of Jesus, the object of our faith is God. God is the only object in the entire universe worthy of worship and devotion and sacrifice, and therefore, the only target worthy of our faith.

Now that we have a basis for our conversation about faith, we have to take this a step further and realize what this implies.

God is not merely the one who calls us to a better life. God **is** the better life we are striving to have.

God is not merely offering us joy and peace and grace in this life. God **is** the joy and peace and grace that our lives need.

Let me get to the point: *If God is not enough, then nothing else will be either.* What we have to recognize is that as we are looking for the things God offers to us because of our relationship with Jesus, we fail to see what God is actually offering to us is himself.

CALLED TO BE WITH GOD

Look at this statement Jesus gave to the disciples in John 15:

> [28] Come to me, all who labor and are heavy laden, and I will give you rest. [29] Take my yoke upon you, and learn from me, for I am gentle and lowly in heart, and

you will find rest for your souls. [30] For my yoke is easy, and my burden is light." (Matthew 11:28-30)

Where is the location Jesus is inviting us to? It is not someWHERE at all, but rather to someONE. "Come to **ME**," Jesus said. Jesus did not mean that in being physically close to him we would find peace and rest. Jesus said that he, in his own person, is the peace and rest, and if we are in a relationship with him we will have what we are longing for.

I will admit, this is not an easy subject to think about or consider. We have to take the time to understand what this means for ourselves. I do not remember who said this first or who said it to me, but it has never left me. It goes like this, "We are so busy looking at God's hands, that we have stopped looking for God's face." I do not know about you, but this is very true of me. I can fall into the "give me" game so easily I forget that what God is interested in is the "with me" game. God wants us to be with him.

This is the sad scene that we referenced in Genesis 3 above. God created paradise, but that was not enough. God gave freedom, but that was not enough. God gave them responsibility, but that was not enough. God gave them pleasure, and that was not enough. God gave himself, and we see that even that did not satisfy the first couple.

Why was it so "easy" to trick and trap Adam and Eve into sin? *It was easy because when we are given everything we want, we think that there is more to be had.* There was nothing missing in Eden. Everything they could have ever wanted was there, but in an attempt to get more they lost it all. We still have not figured that out. We still are trying to exceed the boundaries of God's love and grace by asking for more.

There it is. The great sin is not that Adam and Eve disobeyed God. Please, do not misunderstand me, I am not diminishing this. I am not even saying that this did not happen. The first couple was disobedient. However, the great sin, the sin that was the root cause of their downfall, was that they believed they needed more than what God had provided for them. The great sin was they sought to be satisfied by something other than God. This was the source from which their disobedience manifested itself in rebellion against God.

As we walk this path of faith, we must recognize that faith is not the ever-increasing experiences of new things. Faith is the pure delight in the same thing, in this case, God himself. God is the **only** thing, and he is also everything. Until we really get this, until this becomes the foundational truth that draws us deeper into our relationship with God, we will seek other, more tantalizing diversions. And they are increasing every single day.

Where are you? Have you allowed the interminable opportunities of this world to distract you from the simple joy of fellowship with God? Has your heart been dulled by the constant barrage of stimuli offered to every sense?

What is it that is keeping you distracted from looking forward to those moments spent with God in the "cool of the day"? Until we allow God to satisfy our every need, longing, desire, and appetite we will struggle to live the abundant life Jesus promised. Faith is entirely and unashamedly satisfied with the person of God and nothing else.

❖ ❖ ❖ ❖ ❖ ❖ ❖ ❖

[1] "Moreover, brethren, I declare unto you the gospel which I preached unto you, which also ye have received, and wherein ye stand; [2] By which also ye are saved, if ye keep in memory what I preached unto you, unless ye have believed in vain. [3] For I delivered unto you first of all that which I also received, how that Christ died for our sins according to the scriptures; [4] And that he was buried, and that he rose again the third day according to the scriptures."

1 Corinthians 15:1-4, KJV

❖ ❖ ❖ ❖ ❖ ❖ ❖ ❖

Chapter 11

FAITH IS...

STANDING ON THE WORD OF GOD

I remember the first time I understood the Gospel of Jesus Christ was not just the beginning of the Christian journey but something more. What I know is that when it came to me, I knew (and have known ever since) there was no turning back from that realization. Even attempting to live a life apart from Jesus will never erase the awakening that comes from hearing and understanding the Gospel.

I began to dig deeper into the message of the Gospel. I realized I had not fully allowed myself to be changed and transformed by this good news. In and through the message Jesus proclaimed about himself I began to see how little I really understood. How little I had wanted to know. I had been satisfied with the "get out of jail free" gospel, which is no Gospel at all. Here is, in my estimation, the greatest fact and most profound truth of the Gospel:

The Gospel IS the Christian life.

The Gospel is the beginning; it is the middle; it is the end of the Christian journey. The Gospel allows me in. The Gospel takes me in. The Gospel keeps me in. When we see the Gospel only as an initiation, we are already at a disadvantage. We have already diminished the fullness of the Gospel.

It can be difficult to see how this is true, I will admit that. I had a hard time understanding the richness of this truth. The tendency to seek something "deeper" or more "powerful" beyond the Gospel robs us of the obvious and, many times, most profound realities. Even saying this does not really help to clarify what the Gospel communicates.

Have you ever wondered if it's even possible for there to be anything deeper or more powerful than the Good News of Jesus? Ultimately, our failure to recognize that there is no greater, deeper, or more wonderful spiritual reality than what the Gospel proclaims keeps us held back. It prevents us from seeing what God desires for us to see for ourselves and share with those around us. And worst of all, it stunts our spiritual growth in Christ.

THE GOSPEL ACCORDING TO PAUL

First Corinthians 15:1-4 is, by Paul's admission, the Gospel of Jesus Christ. One of the characteristics I am amazed by in Paul's formulation of the Gospel is that there appear to be details "missing" from what we have commonly come to believe the Gospel is. What I mean is there are many concepts and ideas we have assumed are a part of the Gospel that in fact are not. They are truths and realities we learn and come to understand as effects of the Gospel, but these come after we have received the simple message Paul presented for his readers so they would believe.

There are four key elements Paul says must be present in order for the Gospel to be "THE" Gospel. Those four elements revolve around the death and resurrection of Jesus and only these two events.

1. Christ Died
2. Christ was Buried
3. Christ rose on the third day
4. All this is was done "according to the scriptures."

In the winter of 2008, I conscientiously returned to this simple definition of the Gospel. I have come to believe that Paul's articulation of the Gospel rightly asserts how the redemption of the human soul is not as complicated as we may think. It is profound, of that there can be no question. And it is costly; the cross of Christ illustrates this. But it is not complicated.

The Gospel is veiled in mystery. We have to acknowledge and accept this about God's message to humanity. However, this does not undermine the fact that at the heart of the Christian faith is a miracle of unprecedented proportions and incalculable worth. One that has been debated, argued over and even dismissed by many people in the centuries since Jesus walked with the disciples along the Judean countryside. And despite what people chose to believe or do with the Gospel of Jesus Christ, its claims must be reckoned with by every individual, whether in this life or at the final judgment.

Most Christians do not know how vital Paul's formulation of the Gospel is to how we live. The entire premise of salvation in Christian theology hinges on the resurrection having taken place. If there is no resurrection, there is nothing offered to hell-bound sinners. Paul tells us this much in his explanation that if Jesus did not rise from the grave, then we all should be pitied (1 Corinthians 15:12-19). If any point of the resurrection account is called into question the entire theology of the Christian church falls apart. Let's take a few moments to look at each of these pieces of the Gospel message as Paul conveys it in turn.

1. CHRIST DIED

The first essential element of the Gospel is Jesus' death. There are many who do not believe that Jesus actually died. Various arguments have been given attempting to refute this claim of the Christian faith. Jesus was switched with another person before, during, or after the trial. Jesus was not fully man and therefore, could not be truly killed. Jesus was severely beaten, but he "swooned" or passed out instead of dying. Each of these have been posited as possible explanations for what took place on Golgotha. And each of them intentionally excludes the death of Jesus on the cross.

However, defending the death of Jesus on the cross has been aptly done by others and I will not rehash them here.[22] There are significant historical, theological, and scriptural warrants for believing Jesus was truly and wholly put to death by the Roman executioners. What is pertinent here is that Christ's death was a real death. The reason it was an actual death was because he had an actual birth. The Gospel of Jesus Christ links two of the most unique doctrines in religious thought.

The doctrine of the incarnation serves as the basis that grounds Jesus' own journey upon the earth. Because Jesus was born, Paul can point to the death Jesus experienced on the cross. Without the first, the second does not make any sense. One of the keys to understanding what Paul describes is that the Gospel

---

[22] I recommend *The Case for Christ* by Lee Strobel; *The Case for the Resurrection of Jesus* by Gary R. Habermas and Michael R. Licona; and *Evidence that Demands a Verdict* by Josh McDowell and Sean McDowell as good starting places on the subject.

depends on Jesus enduring the full range of the human experience including, and especially, death.[23]

Trying to understand the mystery of God becoming a man in the person of Jesus of Nazareth has been a point of contention for many as well. To think that God would allow himself to be subjected to the humiliation and horror of death is not something many are willing to accept. *What we have to realize is that if Jesus did not die, we cannot live!* His death had to be real and total. The redemptive promise of God accomplishing our salvation in Christ is fulfilled with the death of the Son on Calvary's cross.

Jesus' death was the fulfillment of all the requirements of the Old Testament's sacrificial system. What the blood of bulls and goats could not do, the blood of Jesus did. In Jesus' death, the need and requirement for sacrifices upon an altar was done away with forever. In

---

[23] The resurrection is pivotal for redemption. This point in undeniable. Included in this discussion, however, should be the matter of the doctrine of incarnation. The resurrection of Jesus and the incarnation of Jesus are inexorably tied to the entire work of redemption. If the resurrection guarantees our redemption, the incarnation introduces our redeemer into the world, providing the means for redemption to take place. This is one of those areas of theology tightly linked to the Gospel, but in Paul's mind at least, does not appear to be a necessary element of the Gospel's presentation. The doctrine of incarnation is beyond the scope of this present work. However, it is important to clarify the equally momentous and theologically significant role the doctrine of incarnation plays in the Gospel. I did not want there to be an over-emphasis on one doctrine without providing some context for another. One of the best books that I have encountered that puts the doctrine of incarnation in proper context is the book by Peter Lewis, *The Glory of Christ* (Chicago: Moody Press, 1997).

Hebrews 10:1-18, we find this idea described. Jesus' sacrifice was the last one offered to God for sin. It was a perfect sacrifice. That is why the death of Jesus is central to the Gospel. This is also why Paul gives it proper prominence in all his writings.

2. CHRIST WAS BURIED

The second essential element of the Gospel has to do with what took place after Jesus' death. One of the more remarkable facts of the crucifixion is that the death of Jesus was like any other human death. Jesus passed from life to death like every other human being before and since, albeit through horrific circumstances. Our Lord's common transition from walking on the earth to being in the presence of the Father provides us with the hope we need to trust that Jesus can lead us through the dark corridor of death.

When we look at the narrative of the crucifixion, there are few details in the Gospels regarding the choice of the Roman soldiers to not break Jesus legs. The reason for breaking the legs of those being executed was to hasten the process of suffocation—the primary cause of death for most who suffered crucifixion.[24] Kenneth O. Gangel describes the situation like this.

---

[24] Craig S. Keener, *The IVP Bible Background Commentary: New Testament* (Downers Grove, IL: InterVarsity Press, 1993), Jn 19:31–33.

"The Romans hastened death by breaking the legs of victims so they would no longer be able to support their bodies. Consequently, the victims' lungs collapsed and they died from suffocation."[25]

After the guards had dispatched of the two thieves on Jesus' left and right hands they came to Jesus. The only reason for not breaking Jesus' legs was because he was already dead.

Lee Strobel, a noted defender of the Christian faith, was a non-believer before beginning a journey to understand and refute the claims of the Bible regarding Jesus. In his book *The Case for Christ,* he interviewed several scholars in various fields of study. One of those interviewed was Dr. Alexander Metherell who possessed two doctorates—one in medicine and another in engineering. During the interview, the moment discussed above came up in the course of the conversation. Doctor Metherell's answer is provided below as it was recorded by Strobel.

"As the person slows down his breathing, he goes into what is called respiratory acidosis—the carbon dioxide in the blood is dissolved as carbonic acid, causing the acidity of the blood to increase. This eventually leads to an irregular heartbeat. In fact, with his heart beating erratically, Jesus would have known

---

[25] Kenneth O. Gangel, *John,* vol. 4, Holman New Testament Commentary (Nashville, TN: Broadman & Holman Publishers, 2000), 353.

that he was at the moment of death, which is when he was able to say, 'Lord, into your hands I commit my spirit.' And then he died of cardiac arrest."[26]

This helps to explain what was happening as Jesus was dying. But, this was not all. Metherell elaborated further on the chain of events that would eventually lead to the cause of death.

"Even before he died—and this is important too—the hypovolemic shock would have caused a sustained rapid heart rate that would have contributed to heart failure, resulting in the collection of fluid in the membrane around the heart, called a pericardial effusion, as well as around the lungs, which is called a pleural effusion."

[Strobel asked,] "Why is that significant?"

"Because of what happened when the Roman soldier came around and, being fairly certain that Jesus was dead, confirmed it by thrusting a spear into his right side. It was probably his right side; that's not certain, but from the description it was probably the right side, between the ribs.

"The spear apparently went through the right lung and into the heart, so when the spear was pulled out, some fluid—the pericardial effusion and the pleural

---

[26] Lee Strobel, *The Case for Christ* (Grand Rapids: Zondervan Publishing House, 1998), 198-199.

effusion—came out. This would have the appearance
of a clear fluid, like water, followed by a large volume
of blood, as the eyewitness John described in his
gospel."[27]

There was no life left in Jesus' body. The Roman
soldiers would have made sure of it. It was the soldiers'
job to ensure their victims were indeed killed. If Jesus'
death were not true, then Jesus would not be able to
provide for us what we need most. This is what
theologians call a substitutionary death. Without Jesus'
intercession and substitution, I would not be able to
experience the fullness of Christ's life in me. If he had not
experienced the pain of death I would have to experience
the full penalty of hell. The reason I can share in Christ's
righteousness is because he fully, completely, and
perfectly shared in what should have been my death. The
fact of his burial points to the certainty of Jesus' death and
agrees with the decision of those present who performed
the burial rite because they believed he needed it.

3. CHRIST ROSE ON THE THIRD DAY

The third element of the Gospel can be succinctly
articulated in the following way: "If Jesus did not come
out of a borrowed grave; there is no hope for anyone to
enter heaven or of fellowship with our heavenly Father."
The importance of the truth of Jesus' death cannot be

---

[27] Ibid., 199.

minimized or diminished. We must work diligently and faithfully to interact with a world that does not believe Jesus' death accomplishes any redemptive work. The message of the Gospel is what sets the Christian faith apart from the teachings of other religions. When we shrink back from this, we surrender the only weapon we have for victory in this life. We exit the only vehicle we have to deliver us to heaven's eternal rest.

Jesus comforted the disciples by telling them he was going to prepare a place for them (John 14:1-3). He was attempting to prepare that original band of leaders for what was coming. The hope Jesus points to is bound to his ability to accomplish and fulfill what he promised. It is in light of this promise that we trust in him as we think about and contemplate our own end. It is in this promise of resurrection, of knowing where he is going, that should work within us an ever-growing hope against the potential despair of the unknown.

When was Jesus going to prepare a place? How long were the disciples going to have to wait? After his death and resurrection. This is why the disciples could not make sense of what Jesus was saying. They wanted to follow Jesus but, Jesus tried to let them know that the path laid out for him was not one they could travel without him going ahead of them first. It was not until after the resurrection that the disciples had a grasp of what was at stake.

The resurrection was the guarantee that every word Jesus taught the disciples was true and would come to pass. The resurrection is the validation of God's word. This is the power of the resurrection.

In raising Jesus from the dead God proves he is faithful to keep his promises to each and every one whom he makes them too. The level of our confidence rises or falls on whether God remains true to his own character. Any deviation would lead to a breakdown in our trust and motivation for fidelity.

4. ALL THIS IS WAS DONE "ACCORDING TO THE SCRIPTURES."

Of the four necessary elements of the Gospel, this last one stands out because it is the one least often mentioned during a presentation of the Gospel. It also stands out because Paul is essentially saying God has staked his reputation, eligibility, and his "worthiness" as God on his ability to predict and fulfill the resurrection. Everything that happened to Jesus happened exactly how God said it would. The trustworthiness of everything the Bible has to say about anything hinges on the resurrection of Jesus having taken place! That seems like a big risk to take unless the resurrection actually happened.

The centrality of the role of revelation contained in the Scriptures in the proclamation of Gospel has been dramatically understated in recent conversations on the subject. Paul was claiming the scriptures serve as their own witness and challenge the reader to confirm its veracity.

Anytime we fail to point out the claims and projections of the Bible regarding the resurrection we inadvertently undermine the place of the Bible in the life of new Christians. If the church does not make the Bible's claims a central aspect of the Gospel, we are undercutting new believers. In the end, what is at stake is the means God has given for communicating to and with his people. If the Bible is unable to accurately relate the events of redemption, then we would be forced to ask in what other areas is it deficient? The resurrection serves as the litmus test for the rest of what the Bible proposes as divine revelation. If the resurrection is true, then everything else is true, even if we do not understand it, or even how to explain it.

Paul intentionally includes the Scriptures as an integral part of Gospel proclamation. As believers and messengers of the Good News, we have to ground our own story in God's story. The Bible is the basis for our testimony. It is what provides the Church with the common ground of faith. It is the glue that binds and bonds believers across ethnic, social, economic, and temporal boundaries. The reason we are surrounded by a great cloud of witness is due to our shared commitment to God's word as the rule for life and faith.

NOTHING LEFT TO CHANCE

The resurrection is not an incidental moment, fact, idea, or detail of the Gospel. Everything the Gospel proclaims and promises rests on the certainty of the resurrection. As believers, we have to consider what this means for us. If the resurrection took place (and it did!), then we all have to live our lives in a manner reflecting this reality. To do otherwise would be disingenuous to our faith and potentially sinful due to our indifference.

As we have journeyed together on this exploration of faith, I have found that many times we do not understand the place of God's Word in the development of faith. God provided his word to us to verify and to support everything he is doing in, through, and around us. Whenever we forgo using the Scriptures as God designed them to be used, we end up finding out that what we are trying to do may not work as well as we had planned or hoped.

I am thankful God has awakened me to this powerful truth. The word of God is not only sufficient for all I need, it was designed to prepare me for every obstacle I might face in living a life of faith. Paul tells Timothy to never lose sight of this amazing reality.

> [16] All Scripture is breathed out by God and profitable for teaching, for reproof, for correction, and for training in righteousness, [17] that the man of God may be complete, equipped for every good work. (2 Timothy 3:16-17)

With each passing day, I grow more convinced that the reason the word of God does not have the effect it describes is not because it does not work, but because we do not allow it to work in us. As followers of Christ and sojourners on this earth, we must strive to live in accord with the word of God. God's word is the only sure source of truth we have. The Scriptures as they have been preserved in the canon of the Old and New Testaments are the only records God has provided to help us get a glimpse of his character, learn of our true plight, and communicate the glorious Gospel that calls all sinners to repentance and salvation in Christ.

It can be easy at times to rely on our emotional intuition to relate to God. However, this is not enough. Our emotions can deceive us. We can be misled and manipulated by our emotions. What God wants to do is to get our mind and our heart to work together. Reading and studying the word are activities of the mind. When these activities are coupled with our hearts, we are able to more actively and more intently live out our faith every day. We must work to rekindle a passion for the word of God so we can stand firmly and steadily upon it.

❖ ❖ ❖ ❖ ❖ ❖ ❖ ❖

[10] So then, as we have opportunity, let us do good to everyone, and **especially to those who are of the household of faith**.

Galatians 6:10 (emphasis added)

❖ ❖ ❖ ❖ ❖ ❖ ❖ ❖

[11] For this is the message that you have heard from the beginning, that we should love one another.

1 John 3:11

❖ ❖ ❖ ❖ ❖ ❖ ❖ ❖

Chapter 12

FAITH IS...

CARING FOR THE PEOPLE OF GOD

My dad served in the United States Army for much of my growing up years. I remember being around soldiers and having the opportunity to hear some of their stories. Soldiers (and all veterans of the armed services really) are an interesting group of people. There are many reasons why these men and women serve. Most of these reasons remain unknown, but one reason I learned over the course of many conversations was the camaraderie that exists among those who serve together. The unit becomes a family and that family becomes supremely important to those who have become a part of it.

This sense of unity can even be seen with older, retired veterans. The banter between the services can be relentless, even on the verge of cruel, and yet, at the end of the day there is this unspoken reality—they have all shared in the experiences of giving of themselves for something greater than their own desires. The Church in many ways mirrors this kind of community because faith is what binds us together; faith in a cause greater than our own lives and comfort; faith in a goal that is worthy of our best efforts. The Church should be the place where individuals can form these lasting bonds of friendship and community. This interconnectedness is what's needed to build a faith community that reflects the heart of God.

THE HEART OF THE CHURCH

Faith is not just what we have inside of us. Faith must find its way out of us into the world in which we live. One of the areas where we must not forget to extend the grace we have received is to those who are a part of our community of faith. Paul plainly tells us we should love one another, and we must not miss the opportunities to "do good" toward those of the "household of faith." It seems clear Paul believed that there was a danger in failing to fulfill this responsibility. As is usually the case, the most familiar things are often the ones most likely to be taken for granted and left untended to.

If we cannot help one another, whom we know and see on a regular basis, how are we ever going to convince anybody else we care for them? What we will inevitably create is a consumption-based relationship. People will come and receive from us because we are willing to give, but a true and deep relationship will not be a part of our time together. The bonds needed for lasting community will never be forged. The heart of the church is the joining of the hearts of its members into a community.

This truth of our faith is an outgrowth of what Jesus taught the disciples. Without a caring Church, there will be no power in the testimony of the Church in and to the world. Jesus' clearest example shows if we are not growing and participating in loving actions toward one another, our witness will amount to very little.

> [34] A new commandment I give to you, that you love one another: just as I have loved you, you also are to love one another. [35] *By this* all people will know that you are my disciples, if you have love for one another. (John 13:34-35, emphasis added)

John makes it clear there is a unique marker of the Christian community. That is why he says, "by this." What was it John was identifying as the evidence of a transformed individual and a true community? It was the love we share for each and among each other. This short phrase—by this—really forces us to consider what we value in our local faith communities. In many of them, we are not living out this ideal.

OUR LOVE IS EVIDENCE OF GOD

Paul also joined John and expanded on this point by letting us know it is possible to fulfill God's law when we love one another as Christ loved us. The idea here is not that we can do now what we could not do before without Jesus. What Paul's statement points to is how the purpose of the law was to help us love one another. Unfortunately, the law had the opposite effect on us. Look at what our love for one another was supposed to achieve.

> [18] Owe no one anything, except to love each other, for the one who loves another has fulfilled the law. (Romans 13:8)

And again, Paul says,

> [10] Love one another with brotherly affection. Outdo one another in showing honor. (Romans 12:10)

John goes so far as to say our love for one another is evidence of the very existence of God when he says,

> [12] No one has ever seen God. But if we love each other, God lives in us, and his love is brought to full expression in us. (1 John 4:12 NLT)

God has chosen to use the bonds of love between members of the body of Christ as evidence of the Gospel, his existence, and his ability to change the human heart. Too often we stop short of saying this. It's almost as if we know, that if we say this, people will give up on the effort.

We cannot make this kind of love up. We have to experience it before we can share it with others.

We should have a genuine fear to become a hindrance to the Gospel. However, we should not also assume that our actions will thwart what God has done. We should not shrink back from striving to love our brothers and sisters in the faith for fear of doing damage to the message of Jesus. We may never love each other perfectly, but that does not mean we should not try at all!

If we understood, accepted, and embraced the power of a loving community as a part of our faith and calling, I believe, much of the bickering we see in our churches would have to stop. But, this would mean we would have to live out the love Jesus demonstrated toward us. We cannot fabricate or fake this kind of love. We cannot behave our way into loving people like Christ loved the church. That is impossible.

Genuine love can only come by way of a radically changed heart. When we are willing to surrender our own desires to do what we want or to choose whom we will love, that is when we begin to love biblically. And this may be where many of us falter. We want to be able to choose whom we love. We have a tendency to fight against being told who we can and cannot love. We can become indignant at the prospect. But, Jesus had something to say about that (Matthew 5:43-48). We do not get to choose who will become a part of our church family. We don't get to pick and choose among them who we are going to love. God has chosen for us.

To Live is Christ

There is a question I now find myself asking regularly. It helps me to clarify my motives and the assumptions I have when I am confronted with a situation I do not like. It is based on Paul's declaration in Galatians 2:20. If you don't know what that verse says, take a minute to look it up. This is the question:

Whose life am I living?

If I do not know how to answer this question, I will not be able to move forward into what God desires for me in my life. What is worse is if I cannot answer this question, I have to ask some other questions about the supposed "change" I claim to have experienced as a result of my profession of faith. There will always be a struggle to live a life of faith. This is natural but, which side appears to have the upper hand? Who keeps winning?

The life of faith we are living requires we take time to investigate and analyze how we are doing. We have to look in the mirror and see if the reflection is that of Jesus or not. It probably will not be easy to admit that we are not really being conformed into Jesus' image. We may not want to accept that, more often than not, we do what we want rather than what God wants. We have just resigned ourselves to living a lie. I do not know what it is for you. I just know the longer I live inconsistently, the greater my deafness to the voice of God and the promptings of the Holy Spirit.

The second verse quoted at the beginning of the chapter makes a subtle claim I do not want us to overlook. John is declaring that the message he and the other disciples took to the nations and the world was and is the same message that was delivered "from the beginning."

It would be somewhat naïve to believe that John was thinking only of Jesus' ministry. John, in his Gospel and in the letters, tends toward an eternal perspective. John, I believe, is pointing us toward the fact God has always desired to express his love toward his creation. But, that is not going far enough. An important component of God's plan was also to have love be the defining reality of all relationships.

Because of the way the Bible describes the connection between our faith in Christ and our love for one another, it is difficult to separate the two—even though some have attempted it. If we claim to have faith in God and there is little-to-no evidence of love for those who are also God's children, we are walking on dangerous ground. John said in his first letter that this is, in essence, an impossibility. If we love God, then we must love one another. We are left with one of two choices. Either we will love one another, or we will live in sin. John simply leaves us no room for an alternative point of view. Look at how he writes it.

> [20] If anyone says, "I love God," and hates his brother,
> he is a liar; for he who does not love his brother whom

he has seen *cannot* love God whom he has not seen.
(1 John 4:20, emphasis added)

Read that verse again. John calls us liars for saying
that we love God and then fail to show love toward our
brothers! The Bible can be uncomfortably rigid when we
read it without any preconceived notions of what it says.
The danger of reading the Bible on its own terms is being
confronted with our own false assumptions and errant
ideas. And then, at that point, we have a choice to make.
We can continue to do what we want. Or, we will submit
to God's word and will for our lives.

We all have to make a choice. We either agree with
God or we do not. We are not free to pick and choose the
parts of the Bible we like and ignore those we dislike. That
option is not available to us. And do you know why?
Because it was not available to Jesus. Even Jesus had to
say to God, "Your will be done." Living a life of faith
demands submission to God's revelation in the Word. If
we are not able, or willing, to submit to what God has said
in his Word, then how can we claim to be willing to
submit in some other area? Or in any other situation?

Based on the verse above, how are you doing? You
cannot at the same time love God and hate your brothers
in the faith. Love is a decisive, intentional action toward
those you see. There is no such thing as "passive" love.
Love is action. Love is movement. Love is alive. Anything
less than this betrays the confession of our mouths about

the condition of our hearts. Love cannot be contained. Love seeks to be expressed.

In closing, I want to offer this prayer for you to consider and pray for yourself. Let it be a guide.

PRAYER FOR GREATER LOVE

Dear Heavenly Father,

Your love for me is perfect. You demonstrated your love by sending Jesus to live, die, be buried and to rise again on the third day. Help me to feel deep within my heart the weight and power and breadth of your love in Jesus. Help me to take what you have put within me by the power of the Holy Spirit and share it with those who are a part of my family of faith. I know I may not always like or approve of what they do but, that does not change that I should love them as Christ loved the church.

Father, help me to prove your love for me by loving others. I no longer want to be a liar. I desire for my life and testimony to agree. The only way this will happen is by trusting in you to transform my heart. I recognize now this is a daily sacrificial act and a life-long process. Give me the strength and courage to surrender to your will, your plan, and your purposes for my life.

In the name of Jesus my Savior, I pray, Amen!

❖ ❖ ❖ ❖ ❖ ❖ ❖ ❖

21 For our sake [God] made [Jesus] to be sin [even though Jesus] knew no sin, so that in [Jesus] we might become the righteousness of God.

2 Corinthians 5:21

❖ ❖ ❖ ❖ ❖ ❖ ❖ ❖

Chapter 13

FAITH IS...

RECEIVING THE RIGHTEOUSNESS OF GOD

I will say this from the start, if you can wrap your mind around what Paul said in 2 Corinthians 5:21 you will be well on your way to living a life that is pleasing to the Lord. If, however, you are like me, and you struggle to make sense of how it could be possible for us to receive the righteousness of God in Christ, I hope you will not give up. I hope you can get a better sense of what it means to be declared righteous, regardless of how we may feel.

One of the great mysteries of the Christian faith is how we, who are despicable sinners, could ever have a relationship with God, who is holy. The chasm that exists between God and us is indescribable and insurmountable. What we have to realize is that even if the gap was the width of a strand of hair, we would not be able to cross it.

Our sin truly creates an obstacle that is theologically and spiritually impassable without divine help.

At the same time, this is possibly one of the most loving and compassionate verses of scripture in the entirety of the Bible. This may appear a stretch in the minds of some after what I said above. Others may even point to other scriptures as better examples of God's love and compassion. I am not offering the final word on the issue. I only want to provide a different point of view. However, I am saying that in this verse we find one of the clearest and simplest statements regarding God's motivation in his work of redemption. Paul's words here reveal the motivation in God's heart toward us in sending Jesus to die for the salvation of repentant sinners.

The broader context of 2 Corinthians 5 is a description of the mission we have been given as disciples. Paul is telling us that as we go out into the world as ambassadors for Jesus, we are supposed to be telling the world what God has done. And the story we are sharing is something so awesome, so mind blowing that if we really thought about it, we would break out into spontaneous praise and worship! The reality of the Gospel is that God is the one doing, not just the heavy lifting, no, God is doing all of the lifting in our salvation.

There are several key points of interest in this ONE verse that we will look at. We will use the "Five W's" many of us learned in grammar school. These are the five interrogative words we will use to help us discover what God has done: Who, What, When, Where, and Why. We will break down how God's grace provides to us the righteousness we need in order to have a relationship with him.

1. WHY?: "FOR OUR SAKE…"

The first question we will look at is this, why did God set his salvation plan into motion? Paul begins with a powerful punch, one that many may be uncomfortable with. The reason God acted in the way that he did; the reason we are the beneficiaries of God's unmerited favor is because God was thinking about us from the beginning. We have to be careful here. Saying this does not make us the center of God's affections. God's primary and ultimate aim is to preserve his name. To proclaim his own glory. He alone is the center of everything.

What Paul describes here is that the reason for Jesus dying was because God knew, understood, and accepted the fact that without Jesus' death there would be no life for anyone. Without God's intervention, no one would escape from the penalty of sin. God's love and grace are the only way to freedom from the effects of sin. Paul wants to leave no doubt regarding our total dependence upon God for salvation.

It was for **OUR** sakes that Jesus came.

It was for **OUR** sakes that Jesus lived.

It was for **OUR** sakes that Jesus died.

It was for **OUR** sakes that Jesus was raised again on the third day.

This is the "why" of Jesus' entire life and ministry on earth. It was for our sakes! This cannot be understated, overstated, minimized, or magnified to a reasonable perspective. What Jesus did is beyond comparison. What Jesus accomplished can never be duplicated. What Jesus did can never be undone.

2. WHO?: "GOD MADE..."

There is nothing in my salvation that can be attributed to my efforts as a sinner. Paul identifies for us the definite and unambiguous performer of the activity of salvation. Paul lets us know who is responsible for the entirety of the salvific endeavor. There is nothing I can contribute to the event or the process.

Salvation is such a precious gift from God he did not and does not see fit to entrust me with any aspect of it. God knows that if I were to lay my hands on his gift of salvation I would do so much damage to it, it would become useless. Not sure how true this is? Look at what Peter has to say on the subject. This is one of the more astonishing passages of scripture in the whole Bible. And, at the same time, it is a wonderful passage of promise!

> [3] Blessed be the God and Father of our Lord Jesus Christ! According to his great mercy, he has caused us to be born again to a living hope through the

resurrection of Jesus Christ from the dead, [4] to an inheritance that is imperishable, undefiled, and unfading, **kept** in heaven for you, [5] who by **God's power are being guarded** through faith for a salvation ready to be revealed in the last time. (1 Peter 1:3-5, emphasis added)

The wonder of God's love is that he secures the grace and the salvation he provides. He is unwilling for anyone to lose what he has carefully provided through the death of his Son. God does not even trust anyone to maintain it. God does that himself. This is grace through and through, from beginning to end.

3. HOW?: "MADE [JESUS] TO BE SIN [EVEN THOUGH JESUS] KNEW NO SIN..."

In this clause, Paul raises one of the great theological puzzles of the Christian faith. How is it that God has provided for us what we needed to be redeemed more than anything else, his righteousness? The Scripture says Jesus was made to be sin. The idea is that Jesus became sin. Not that Jesus committed a sin; not that Jesus sinned, but that somehow he became the very thing I am, without actually being guilty of doing anything wrong.

I think you are beginning to see the difficulties here. How is this possible? There is a concept we have to grapple with to make sense of what Paul wrote. It is described by a big word but is can be understood rather easily. The concept is imputation. According to Ryrie's

Basic Theology, "to impute means to attribute or reckon or ascribe something to someone."[28] Allow me to offer an illustration. I love to smear butter on a freshly baked dinner roll. The butter is not a part of the roll, but when I take the knife and I apply the butter, I have imputed the butter to the dinner roll.

This is the idea. Jesus did not change who he was, but something was added to him that was not his, the flesh of humanity in his incarnation. The reality of this addition made it possible for Jesus to experience the effects of the fall. The one remaining problem was that because of Jesus' purity he would never sin. So, this obstacle of Jesus' moral perfection had to be overcome somehow. Because how was a perfect human being, who was not tainted by sin, going to die? The only way to accomplish this would be to have Jesus killed.

It was through the murder of the Son of God that the penalty of the sin of the whole world was applied to Jesus. This is why Paul says that God made Jesus to be sin, because if God had not counted humanity's sin against Jesus, Jesus could not and would not have died. Physical death is the statutory penalty for sin. In order for Jesus to be our substitute and redeem us from the very sin that was condemning us to hell, he had to experience death. This is the miracle of Jesus' life. Jesus becomes/became sin

---

[28] Charles Caldwell Ryrie, *Basic Theology: A Popular Systematic Guide to Understanding Biblical Truth* (Chicago, IL: Moody Press, 1999), 256.

in his death because he could not sin because he did not possess a sin nature.

Peter Lewis in his great book by, *The Glory of Christ*, speaks to the centrality of Jesus's person to the Christian faith. In it, he writes these fantastic few sentences describing what was taking place when Jesus showed up on the scene as a human being.

> "It comes to this: for our salvation it is as necessary that the Son of God be truly and fully human as that He be truly and fully divine. If this humanity is less than full and true, then he is inadequate as a mediator, incompetent as a sympathizer and disqualified as a redeemer. If (save for sin) He is not all that we are in our uttermost humanity, the He cannot perfectly represent us either in His life or in His death. If He does not descend to us from God, the He cannot lift us up to God."[29]

The wonder and mystery of the incarnation is the linchpin that makes our redemption possible and sure. In the incarnation, God paved the way to the cross, and at the cross, Jesus became guilty of something he never did himself, your and my sin. The incarnation is how our redemption is procured.

---

[29] Peter Lewis, *The Glory of Christ* (Chicago: Moody Press, 1997), 142.

4. WHERE?: "SO THAT IN [JESUS]..."

As we move from the "Why" to the "Who" and pass through the "How," we arrive at the "Where." Where is it God places us after Jesus has taken our place on the cross? This short clause packs a powerful punch in answering that for us. Listen to where God has put us. God has put us in Jesus! But how can he do that? He can do it because that was the plan was from the beginning. Those two words, "so that," right there are the arrows pointing to God's design. However, what do those two words mean for us? Based on what we have already seen, what they mean is that what comes after *IS GUARANTEED!*

Do not miss that. Do not read this truth and just pass along as if something ordinary has happened!

This is the power of what is being declared here in this verse. The reason God is able to give to us what rightfully belongs to Jesus is because Jesus took from us what rightly belonged to us and made it his own. We are heading toward heaven because Jesus punched the ticket with a blood-soaked nail. This is not a cheap fare. The Gospel moves us from the Glory of God to the Grace of God on a clear and direct path. The journey from glory to grace goes right through the terrible door of the Judgment of God, and that judgment fell directly upon Jesus.

The second part of this clause highlights that all of this takes place "in Jesus." And right at this point is where true Christianity is separated from all other religions, philosophical systems, and ideologies of the world. If a person does not come to Jesus, trust in Jesus, hold to Jesus and rely on Jesus, all of the benefits of God's righteousness cannot be enjoyed. And what's worse, they will never be applied to the sinner's account.

Salvation in Christ *is* conditional. All of salvation depends on our staying in Jesus and only Jesus. And at the same time, it is unconditional because what God provides he also sustains.

5. WHAT?: "WE MIGHT BECOME THE RIGHTEOUSNESS OF GOD."

This is the great truth of the Gospel. The Gospel, I believe, answers this question: What is the ultimate goal of God's redemption plan? The Gospel preaches Christ was crucified, buried, and raised so that we may become sons and daughters of God; so that we might become heirs and joint heirs with Jesus. So that we might be transformed in our minds, conformed into the image of Jesus, and renewed by the Holy Spirit in every area of life. However, all of this presupposes that we are now something different. That the condition that keeps us alienated from God has been rectified. That what we have become has changed. FOREVER!

One of the most excellent reasons we have for rejoicing in this walk of faith is coming to grips and reveling in the fact that God's plan for salvation was not an afterthought. God knew what it was going to take to redeem a fallen human race. And, Jesus willingly stepped down from his thrown at the right hand of God and stepped into the finite, fallen world of sinners. At the heart of this act of undefiled love is the understanding that without sacrifice the price of salvation would never have been paid. Without Jesus' death, there is no imputed righteousness. Without the cross, there is no hope. And without faith in Jesus, there should not be any expectation of enjoying the benefits of God's grace. This is both the hard truth and the tender reality of the Gospel. We are saved but on God's terms, in God's way. Without exception.

CONCLUSION

Faith in Christ, the kind of faith that sets a person free from sin, fear, and all of the traps that lead to bondage, can only come when we freely receive the righteousness of God. It is not something that can be won, earned, or coerced. It must be enjoyed, plain and simple. To do otherwise is to jeopardize living into the full reality of God's grace. Don't make that mistake.

Receive what has been given and then do what you should be doing already, leave it in God's hands.

❖ ❖ ❖ ❖ ❖ ❖ ❖ ❖

³ The Son radiates God's own glory and expresses the very character of God…

Hebrews 1:3a

❖ ❖ ❖ ❖ ❖ ❖ ❖ ❖

²⁹ For those whom he foreknew he also predestined to be conformed to the image of his Son, in order that he might be the firstborn among many brothers.

Romans 8:29

❖ ❖ ❖ ❖ ❖ ❖ ❖ ❖

² Dear friends, now we are children of God, and what we will be has not yet been made known. But we know that when Christ appears, we shall be like him, for we shall see him as he is. ³ All who have this hope in him purify themselves, just as he is pure.

1 John 3:2-3, NIV

❖ ❖ ❖ ❖ ❖ ❖ ❖ ❖

Chapter 14

FAITH IS...

RADIATING THE GLORY OF GOD

My wife and I were still in college and still dating when we went to Metter, Georgia, the home of Dr. Michael Guido. Dr. Guido was an evangelist and the founder of Sower Ministries. The headquarters to his ministry was in this small South Georgia community and we were told that if we ever had the chance we should go over and see the grounds.

The complex housed the publishing operation of the ministry, a beautiful garden, and it also served as Dr. and Mrs. Guido's home. It was an amazing place tucked away into a rural community. You would never think of finding a ministry with a worldwide influence there.

We arrived and told the secretary that we were just visiting. We were from Statesboro, a community about thirty-five minutes away and just wanted to look around. She graciously offered to give us a tour of the facilities and we told her that would be much appreciated. She proceeded to provide us with a history of the ministry and of the property. After about twenty minutes we were told that everything that we had seen had at one time been on the ministry's prayer board and was ultimately donated to the effort. My wife and I were stunned by this revelation. We were taken to the conference room where the prayer board was hanging. My wife and I exchanged a look because we saw that there were several items on that list that cost a significant amount of money.

As we continued the tour, we happened to see Dr. Guido driving the grounds on his golf cart. (Something we were informed he did regularly.) The secretary asked if we had ever met Dr. Guido. We said he had not, but we had just seen him driving around. We chuckled. She then proceeded to go into his office and ask if we could visit for a few minutes. We told her we did not want to inconvenience him, but she assured us it was all right. She emerged from his office a minute later and walked us in.

What happened next, I did not expect, and I have not experienced in the same way again. I have heard of going into a place where the presence of God seems to dwell, but I had never actually known what it meant until I met this elderly saint. The only way I can explain what happened is that it felt as if I was no longer on earth. It was as if I had been instantly transported to another place. There was a heaviness to the air in the office. There was an undeniably tangible and physical dimension to the atmosphere. I am not saying there was something particularly special about the man as I looked at him, but there indeed was something different about this man. We spent about ten minutes with him. He prayed with us and then we left.

This was the first time I had ever met someone with whom I had the distinct impression they knew something about God that I did not know. As my wife and I left that afternoon, I was sure of two things. First, there was a man in Metter, Georgia, who walked with God. Second, I wanted to have what he undeniably had in abundance.

DREAMS OF A PERFECT LIFE

I love movies. One of my favorite things to do is to sit down and watch a film that has been recommended by a friend. I am not a critic, but I have noticed that the human mind needs to resolve inconsistencies and contradictions. Otherwise, we get frustrated with the story we are told. I have also noticed that, in general, most movies do not end on a sour note. There may be many turns and twists in the plot and even moments where the solution seems impossible. But, ultimately the ending resolves and the tensions and anxieties that were felt by the viewer go away. There is a sense of satisfaction that comes over us as spectators. We expect there to be a resolution. What excites us is the discovery of how the pressure in the story will be released.

Life can have a similar tendency. It does not really matter how or why but there is a desire for life to have purpose, meaning, and direction. When this unified view of life is not present, we become discouraged and despondent. As human beings, we need to "know" that everything will work out in the end. When life appears to not be heading toward resolution, we being to lose hope.

For many of us who claim to follow Jesus, we also have this expectation. However, many times we simply cannot recognize how all of the pieces to the faith puzzle will work together or what picture will emerge. The question that haunts our hearts can be expressed in the following way.

What is the purpose, goal, and ultimate end of this life of faith?

I think we could come up with a comprehensive and varied list of answers to the question. And, I do not believe any of those answers would be wrong or inappropriate. What I might say is many of our responses could potentially be too shallow to accurately represent how God actually sees us.

God's ultimate purpose for his people must be higher and grander than anything we could ever conceive on our own. To think otherwise might be somewhat naïve or even pessimistic on our part. If God's purposes for his children are something we could conjure up in our own minds and hearts we would be able to count ourselves equal to God, even if only in regard to our purpose.

The power of God to transform us from what we are to what he intends for us to be is something truly amazing. I say this, and I know that I do not fully understand what I am attempting to describe. Just imagining a time in my future where I will be perfect is difficult. Where every action, thought, and word will be correct. Thinking about a time when I will no longer be the source of pain or suffering to those I care for most. That I will no longer make a mistake in judgment that will bring about negative or unintended consequences to those I have never met. This truly is a wonderful thought. I can only dream about what that will be like.

Over the course of this book, my hope has been to expand our understanding of what faith is. Knowing what something is can help us to live better and choose better. But, faith is not like most other subjects. Faith, unlike many other aspects of life, is something that comes from God and works its way through us. Faith is dependent on the object we are expressing faith in. It is impossible to have faith in nothing. That is a contradiction in ideas. Faith must always point to something outside of itself.

GOD IS THE GIVER OF FAITH

What I have come to realize is that our faith, this faith in Jesus we claim, is not something that we strive for.

While there are times we can talk about pushing into our faith or holding onto faith, the Christian faith is of a different nature. Faith in Christ takes hold of us, it pulls us forward, and it calls us to go deeper. Christian faith is not fabricated from within the heart or formulated in the mind. Christian faith is poured in from without because the object of our faith is so compelling, so transforming, that it provokes action as we interact with God, the source of our faith.

This begs the question, **"Why do we not see this 'compelling' drive more often in those of us that profess faith in Jesus?"**

I think one primary reason we fail to see this drive is we have not accepted the reality of one of the most essential effects faith has in our lives. The effect I am referring to is that God desires to make us like Christ in every way. This is not an afterthought in God's plan. Becoming like Jesus is the ultimate goal of God for every one of his children. In order to understand this, we must orient our minds so we know that one of the primary reasons we are made like Christ is so we can radiate the very glory of God to world. At no point on this faith journey are we to point to ourselves or seek to highlight our own glory over God's.

Fundamentally, when our chief aim is not the glory of God we cannot claim to have at the center of our lives what Jesus had at the center of his. Everything Jesus did he did because that was exactly what God wanted him to do. Everything Jesus said was exactly what God wanted him to say. Jesus and God were so close together Jesus described the relationship between himself and the Father as being one (John 10:30). I can understand some of the theological realities this statement was pointing to, however, it would be a terribly shortsighted perspective to dismiss the relational reality Jesus was describing for us as well.

Jesus' Desire For His Disciples

Do you remember Jesus' prayer for the disciples and all disciples to follow? Jesus prayed that we would all be one. What did Jesus use as a comparable example of what he was thinking? In order to help his disciples understand what he wanted, Jesus turned to the relationship he shared with God the Father. My relationship with my brothers and sisters of faith ought to be just like Jesus' relationship with God the Father. John captured Jesus' prayer on this issue and recorded it in John 17:

> [20] "I am praying not only for these disciples but also for all who will ever believe in me through their message. [21] I pray that they will all be one, just as you and I are one—as you are in me, Father, and I am in you. And *may they be in us* so that the world will believe you sent me.

> [22] "I have given them the glory you gave me, so they may be one as we are one. [23] I am in them and you are in me. May they experience such perfect unity that the world will know that you sent me and that you love

them as much as you love me. [24] Father, I want these whom you have given me to be with me where I am. Then they can see all the glory you gave me because you loved me even before the world began!

[25] "O righteous Father, the world doesn't know you, but I do; and these disciples know you sent me. [26] I have revealed you to them, and I will continue to do so. Then your love for me will be in them, and I will be in them." (John 17:20-26 NLT, emphasis added)

I highlighted one phrase, but the entire passage is so rich with implications regarding God's desires for us. God is looking and working for us to become like his Son because of our faith in him. Just read and re-read that passage a couple of times and see how Jesus joins together, not only his life with the Father's but also how Jesus serves as the means for joining our lives with God's life. Jesus prayed and was crucified to make it possible for us to have a real and vibrant relationship with our heavenly Father.

It is this unifying aspect of faith that magnifies the intensity of God's glory in us. Those outside the body of Christ will see a fuller picture of who God is because of how we come together. We cannot adequately show God's glory as he deserves as individuals. There are shimmers of it within each of us because we are created in the image of God. But, in order for the world to get the clearest picture possible, we must come together. This is the mystery revealed in the gathered community of believers called the Church. When the Church gathers together, the fullness of God's glory is being put on display for all to see.

Everything God desires for the Son, he desires to see in those who are becoming like Jesus. The closer we draw to Jesus and the closer we walk with Jesus, the more like him we will become. The more we become like Jesus, the more capacity we will have in radiating the glory of God to the world.

❖ ❖ ❖ ❖ ❖ ❖ ❖ ❖

[50] Before the year of famine came, two sons were born to Joseph. Asenath, the daughter of Potiphera priest of On, bore them to him. [51] Joseph called the name of the firstborn Manasseh. "For," he said, "God has made me forget all my hardship and all my father's house." [52] The name of the second he called Ephraim, "For God has made me fruitful in the land of my affliction."

Genesis 41:50-52

❖ ❖ ❖ ❖ ❖ ❖ ❖ ❖

[20] You intended to harm me, but God intended it for good to accomplish what is now being done, the saving of many lives.

Genesis 50:20 NIV

❖ ❖ ❖ ❖ ❖ ❖ ❖ ❖

Chapter 15

FAITH IS...

RECOGNIZING THE HAND OF GOD

One of my favorite biblical stories is found in the book of Esther. The story is about Esther, a simple and humble Jewish girl, who ends up carried away by the circumstances of her day. She inadvertently finds herself in one of the most pivotal moments in the history of her people.

She had no idea Queen Vashti would stand against King Xerxes, nor could she have anticipated she would find favor with the king or be selected to be the next queen. Esther could never have predicted the racism that would motivate Haman, the king's closest advisor, to attempt genocide by way of treachery. The intrigue and scandal of this story have the marks of a great movie plot. However, what makes this story stand out is how difficult it was for Esther to see what God was trying to do through her for God's people.

There is another character in this story that provides the perspective we need. Esther's uncle and caretaker, Mordecai, helps her see that her rise to prominence was not merely for her benefit. God did not bless her so she could enjoy living in the lap of luxury while God's people fell to Haman's plan. Mordecai's words have become legendary. They are profound and pointed. The call to action he extends to his niece should serve as a reminder to all of us that there are realities and responsibilities more important than life itself; a lesson Esther quickly learned.

When Mordecai comes to Esther and lays out Haman's devious plot, Esther rebuts by explaining palace protocol. Mordecai will have none of this. He reminds her that regardless of her position in the king's court she will not escape what is to come.

> [13] ..."Don't think for a moment that because you're in the palace you will escape when all other Jews are killed. [14] If you keep quiet at a time like this, deliverance and relief for the Jews will arise from some other place, but you and your relatives will die. Who knows if perhaps you were made queen for just such a time as this?"

> [15] Then Esther sent this reply to Mordecai: [16] "Go and gather together all the Jews of Susa and fast for me. Do not eat or drink for three days, night or day. My maids and I will do the same. And then, though it is

against the law, I will go in to see the king. If I must die, I must die." (Esther 4:13-16 NLT)

Mordecai's role in Esther's life was to point to the hand of God at work. His now famous words have been used to remind others that, many times, we are not given the opportunity to choose the circumstances we find ourselves in. In spite of this, we all must take hold of what is in front of us and choose to do what we can. God's plans are perfect. They just are not always plain for us see.

WHY ARE WE SURPRISED WHEN WE SUFFER?

In this chapter, we are not going to be looking at how the Bible, or the Christian faith for that matter, addresses the suffering of others. What I want to look at is what the Bible has to say about the way that a Christian *should* suffer in light of the faith we profess in Jesus.

Please know from the start, I think we all should see suffering as an expected reality of life. The assumption of suffering is the perspective of many of the writers of the scriptures, including Jesus. I think one of the more difficult thoughts we have to overcome is this: as Christians, we can fall for the often told, or implied, lie that suffering will no longer be a part of our lives once we profess faith in Jesus. And if there is suffering, it is because of some moral failure, some lesson God wants us to learn, or it is something that just happens to us because of the devil and then God will swoop in and will somehow make things all right in the end.

When we frame suffering in these ways, we risk developing a deficient theology of suffering and, to our harm, we end up undermining God's character in the process. When we do not understand suffering as something to expect in our lives, we hold onto a view of God inconsistent with the Bible's testimony. Not only that, we start to create all sorts of terrible alternatives that are also inconsistent to how a Christian should respond to or understand suffering. I often find the responses to suffering mentioned above to be shallow, hurtful, and inconsistent with what the Bible says on the subject. What makes matters more amazing is that, as the Church, we have not investigated deeply enough what God, Jesus, and the writers of the Old and New Testaments have to teach us about suffering both theologically and practically.

I have come to realize that many believers' have a theology of suffering that is incompatible with what the Bible teaches. It might even be safe to say that their theology is contrary to what the Bible teaches. Period. What this leads to is a self-centered view of suffering, the avoidance of difficult circumstances and choices, and an unwillingness to be instruments of God's glory regardless of what happens to us and especially when the seas of life become turbulent.

This chapter will not answer all of the questions about suffering in the world. That is not the purpose. Our goal is to help us reorient our thinking to a more biblical one on the subject. Hopefully, this will help us avoid some of the frustrations we may feel on the subject of suffering. We will now turn our attention toward several scriptures that will help us determine a biblical response to suffering.

SOME RIDICULOUS VERSES

The question we want to answer is this: **What does the bible say about how a Christian should suffer?** I will not attempt to capture the whole of the scriptures witness on the issue of Christian suffering, however, I would like to provide a representative sample. This will help us to understand how Christian's are supposed to accept, receive, and understand suffering. And then, after entering into suffering how we should respond to be consistent with the biblical witness.

The story of Joseph is one of the best representations in the Bible of how to respond to suffering. Joseph is standing in a position of power and his brothers, the ones who sold him into a life of misery, are now standing before him. There would be no greater opportunity to exact his revenge if that were what he really wanted to do. But that is not how Joseph sees the situation. Joseph has come to understand that God's purpose for his life was far different from what even his brothers could have known. Joseph looked at them and said, "You intended to harm me, but **God intended it all for good**. He brought me to this position so I could save the lives of many people" (Genesis 50:20 NLT, emphasis added). The question that we should ask ourselves is this: Would you or I have enough insight and faith to see this for ourselves?

How could Joseph have said this? The only way to make sense of it is to assume Joseph had come to see the circumstances of his life as being orchestrated by a hand far beyond himself. That what he had endured were the necessary steps of God's will in his life so God's glory would be seen in the world. For some of us, this is a very difficult pill to swallow. I can understand and appreciate that. But, listen to how Jesus described the world's disdain for his disciples.

> [18] If the world hates you, know that it has hated me before it hated you. [19] If you were of the world, the world would love you as its own; but because you are not of the world, but I chose you out of the world, therefore the world hates you. [20] Remember the word that I said to you: 'A servant is not greater than his master.' If they persecuted me, they will also persecute you. If they kept my word, they will also keep yours. [21] But all these things they will do to you on account of my name, because they do not know him who sent me. (John 15:18-21)

If there is anyone else in the scripture who understood what Jesus meant about the animosity that the world would have toward Christians it was the apostle Paul. I want to share a few passages that are just mind-blowingly odd, not because of what they describe, but in the way that Paul thought about the suffering he personally endured. Notice the connections he made between what was happening and how he understood what was happening.

> [3] More than that, *we rejoice* in our sufferings, *knowing* that suffering produces endurance, [4] and endurance produces character, and character produces hope, [5] and hope does not put us to shame, because God's love has been poured into our hearts through the Holy Spirit who has been given to us. (Romans 5:3-5)

> [16] The Spirit himself bears witness with our spirit that we are children of God, [17] and if children, then heirs — heirs of God and fellow heirs with Christ, provided we suffer with him *in order that* we may also be glorified with him. [18] For I consider that the sufferings of this present time are *not worth comparing with the glory that is to be revealed to us*. (Romans 8:16-18, emphasis added)

Who talks like this? Seriously! How can you look at the suffering you are undergoing and not become bitter or hardened by it? There is only one answer. Paul had become convinced of **EVERY** word Jesus taught. There were no reservations. There was no doubt. There was nothing that could distract this apostle from the task laid before him.

Peter provides us with some more peculiar verses. In his first letter, Peter provides us with two helpful passages that further place how we view suffering for

Christ in their proper context. Take note of the way that rejoicing and suffering are tied together.

> 12 Beloved, *do not* be surprised at the fiery trial when it comes upon you to test you, *as though something strange* were happening to you. 13 *But rejoice* insofar as you share Christ's sufferings, that you may also rejoice and be glad when his glory is revealed. 14 If you are *insulted* for the name of Christ, *you are blessed*, because the Spirit of glory and of God rests upon you. … 16 Yet if anyone suffers as a Christian, let him not be ashamed, but let him glorify God in that name. (1 Peter 4:12-14, 16, emphasis added)

Many of us do not normally think like this. In fact, most of us would never think like this. This may be part of the problem. The following passage addresses the way suffering bonds us together because of our connected faith to Jesus.

> 9 Resist him, firm in your faith, knowing that the same kinds of suffering are being experienced by your brotherhood throughout the world. 10 And *after you have suffered a little while*, the God of all grace, who has called you to his eternal glory in Christ, will himself restore, confirm, strengthen, and establish you. (1 Peter 5:9-10, emphasis added)

There are more examples in the Scriptures that support this mindset because, in the end, that's what we are talking about. We are talking about a change in the way we think about the suffering we endure on this journey of faith. This change is not easy. But it only gets harder when we fight against the testimony of God's word on the subject.

SUFFERING MAY NOT BE A CURSE

Suffering as a Christian is one of the marks and one of the evidences that we are pressing into the enemy's territory. When we become satisfied with the way things are; when we are comfortable with the events that are taking place around us, we have not fully grasped the power and intensity of the Gospel. Why do I make such a statement? I say this for one simple reason. A reason Paul himself offered up for his devotion and single-minded tenacity in spreading the message of Jesus: *he believed the Good News was worthy of being spread to as many as would receive it*.

As I think about my journey of faith, I wonder, "Have I loved and lived the Gospel in such a way that my life becomes more difficult, not less?" This is the reality of a life redefined by the Gospel. When we are convinced of the Gospel everything changes, especially the way we think about life. The following verse from Romans 9 is one of the best examples of this kind of radical change of thinking.

[3] For I could wish that I myself were **accursed and cut off from Christ** *for the sake* of my brothers, my

kinsmen according to the flesh. (Romans 9:3, emphasis added)

We have just hit the twilight zone of Bible verses. I have read this verse often and I still know I do not fully understand the magnitude of what Paul was saying. Paul seems to be saying that when he looked at his countrymen, the Jews, his love for them was so strong he was willing to forsake the single most precious thing he had. To say it another way, Paul is saying he, if he were able to, would choose to endure the fires of hell and eternal torment "for the sake of" his countrymen!

The longing of his heart; the depth of his love, the tenderness of his ministry was always for one thing, that others might come to know Jesus. If that meant being jailed, beaten, stoned, almost drown, or chased out of town, then suffering would be worth the cost. The Gospel was such Good News to Paul's soul and mind that anything and everything was worth enduring so Jesus would be proclaimed.

Here are several other passages that continue to put suffering, not in the category of a curse, but rather the blessed opportunity of every believer to make Jesus known to the world. These passages speak for themselves and will not be accompanied with any commentary to follow.

> [7] But whatever gain I had, I counted as loss for the sake of Christ. [8] Indeed, I count everything as loss

because of the surpassing worth of knowing Christ Jesus my Lord. For his sake I have suffered the loss of all things and count them as rubbish, in order that I may gain Christ … [10] that I may know him and the power of his resurrection, and may share his sufferings, becoming like him in his death… (Philippians 3:7-8, 10, emphasis added)

[20] I have been crucified with Christ. *It is no longer I who live,* but Christ who lives in me. And the life I now live in the flesh I live by faith in the Son of God, who loved me and gave himself for me. (Galatians 2:20, emphasis added)

[8] Therefore *do not be ashamed* of the testimony about our Lord, nor of me his prisoner, but share in suffering for the gospel by the power of God, … [12] which is why I suffer as I do. But **I am not ashamed**, *for I know whom I have believed,* and *I am convinced* that he is able to guard until that Day what has been entrusted to me. (2 Timothy 1:8, 12, emphasis added)

[19] *For this is a gracious thing,* **when, mindful of God,** *one endures sorrows while suffering unjustly.* [20] For what credit is it if, when you sin and are beaten for it, you endure? But if when you do good and suffer for it you endure, this is a gracious thing in the sight of God. [21] *For to this you have been called,* because Christ also suffered for you, leaving you an example, *so that you might follow in his steps.* [22] He committed no sin, neither was deceit found in his mouth. [23] When he was reviled, he did not revile in return; when he

suffered, he did not threaten, but continued entrusting himself to him who judges justly. [24] He himself bore our sins in his body on the tree, that we might die to sin and live to righteousness. By his wounds you have been healed. (James 2:19-24, emphasis added)

OPPORTUNITIES WASTED

One of the thoughts that runs through my mind after reading verses like these is wondering, how many opportunities I have wasted? Opportunities where I was faced with a difficult situation, and rather than turning to God to sustain me through it I blamed him for what I was dealing with. When we don't know what to do, we do what feels right. The danger with this approach to life is that our feelings are never fully informed of all that is happening around us. So, when we depend on such an unreliable source of information, we make decisions and entertain thoughts that are not congruent or consistent with God's word and plan for us.

Suffering, not pleasure, strengthens our faith. Suffering forces us to depend upon God to sustain us in the midst of our trials. While pleasure has the opposite effect, driving all of our attention and affections inward. When this happens, we lose sight of almost everything around us. I guess the question becomes this: Why do we run from suffering so quickly?

I am not advocating we wallow in misery or that we put ourselves into foolish and dangerous situations. I would advise the opposite. Live in wisdom. Live fully aware of the world in which we make our lives. But, don't be surprised if a faithful life causes others to resent our convictions and desires to live in accordance to God's design.

What I am wondering is why don't we see—or maybe we just can't see—how God could use suffering for his glory. The underlying assumption here is that God would not allow suffering to happen to us. That God will protect us from the world and its influences. This can be a misguided and precarious place to walk.

We may be better served to become convinced of this simple truth—that we will not be shielded from trouble. Then we may find ourselves driven to the Gospel, into the arms of our Savior, and we will no longer find our satisfaction in the small and dissipating pleasures this world offers.

STRIVE FOR WHAT IS BETTER

Once we get to the point where we recognize that our faith will not insulate us from suffering in this world, we will begin to see how the Gospel prepares us to endure suffering. This will cause a shift in how we understand what passionately living out the Gospel does to the heart and mind of a follower of Jesus. Peter again is helpful here.

¹⁷ "For it is better to suffer for doing good, if that should be God's will, than for doing evil." (1 Peter 3:17)

¹⁹ "Therefore let those who suffer according to God's will entrust their souls to a faithful Creator while doing good." (1 Peter 4:19)

Peter seems to just come out and say it. There may be times when suffering **IS** included as a part of God's plan for us. Notice carefully what I said. Suffering may be a part of God's plan, not the intentional product of God's will. This is an important distinction. God is not the author of evil. He cannot sin. Therefore, we need an expanded understanding of God's character to make sense of this.

When we are talking about difficult topics, we must never impugn the character of God. We must never call into question God's motives. Our limited and incomplete point of view hinders our ability to see all that is happening. Our limited cognitive faculties cannot hold all of the data involved in calculating the governance of the universe. When we make a judgment of God's judgment we have embarked on a fool's errand. We have made a terrible mistake; one that will lead us away from God each and every time.

Now, I will admit how God knowing that suffering will happen in our lives may sound *wrong* to us. There are actually many within the Christian community who teach and believe this would never happen and should not even be entertained. But, they do this in contradiction to what the Bible plainly says. The suffering of the saints is an inconvenient truth. One we have to deal with honestly. The reality of what God says in his word, however, should trump our own thoughts and ideas on the matter, rather than trying to make the Scriptures say something they do not say.

While there may be times in our lives where we live in fear that suffering may come, we should remember God is fully aware of all that is taking place around us. There is nothing that escapes God's observing eyes. If we believe in God's love; if we believe in God's grace; if we believe God will work all things out for our good, then we have to be careful not to make every experience of suffering into a time to complain and gripe and doubt God's plan. If and when we suffer, we must make sure that we suffer justly. We should consider the fact that we do not suffer *more* the true miracle of God's love.

The question I would suggest should be taking shape as we consider suffering in light of what the Bible says is this:

Can I worship God if the suffering I endure IS because of something in God's plan, which God has chosen not to stop or reveal it to me?

When we think about what is happening around us, it can be so easy to lose sight of the greatness and grandeur of God. But, suffering has a way of adjusting our focus. If suffering happens as a part of God's will then we have no reason to fear. We can trust God will see us through. However, if we take the opposite view, the view that suffering occurs without God's knowledge, there is also a dark reality we have to address. If suffering happens outside of God's will we are left to the mercy of circumstances that exist beyond God's control. This is not a palatable position to take nor is it an idea the Bible even allows for. It is totally inconsistent with divine revelation.

So, what do we do when we are confronted with the possibility, and according to Peter, the actuality that suffering may be a part of God's plans? Will we retreat from what the Bible says, or will we allow God to shape our view of the world? Because suffering has such a clarifying effect on us, we will have a wide variety of assumptions we may be holding confronted. Assumptions we may have made about how God works in the world that may not be correct at all. These are assumptions that must be changed if we are going to live in obedience to God and his word.

The challenge Peter sets before us is this: when we find ourselves reeling from the concussion that suffering inflicts on our lives and heart, will we be able to "entrust [our] souls to a faithful Creator?" A *faithful* Creator. God's faithfulness toward us should never be called into question. As pilgrims on the journey of faith, we need to trust that God's purposes for the events and circumstances of history are superintended and guarded against sabotage by his sovereign reign.

In the end, there is one truth we must never allow to drift too far from our minds. It is captured in the words of John to his children in the faith. It is a lesson that we should all strive to internalize and live out each and every day. The truth is that we should not expect the world to love us or accept us when what we believe is contrary to the trajectory of the world.

> [13] Do not be surprised, brothers, that the world hates you. (1 John 3:13)

This is the reality of our faith. This is the call to which we have been called as the body of Christ. This is the mission that ought to push us to a greater commitment to advance the Gospel and extend the Kingdom of God. These efforts should be done with a clear understanding of what it will cost us personally as we forge ahead.

Additional Passages to Consider: 2 Corinthians 1:5-6; Galatians 6:17; Philippians 1:21, 29; Colossians 1:24; Hebrews 5:8; James 1:2-3; 1 Peter 3:14-17

FAITH IS...

AN ONGOING JOURNEY TOWARD HOME

Many of my fears regarding the study of faith are based on my desire to avoid a common misconception about what it means to have faith in the first place. It is a notion that has been created in the minds of some within the Christian community. This idea is that the world and the Church must become more aligned here on earth. It is the belief that heaven can be, or even should be brought to the earth. This point of view is based on the false assumption that this is God's plan for his people and the world. If the truth were told, the only reason that heaven even manifests itself on earth is because Kingdom people—the saints of God—roam the landscape as sojourners and ambassadors.

We are the ones who bring heaven to earth through our faithful living, not by trying to recreate it. If creating heaven on earth were God's intended plan, Jesus would not have left and returned to heaven to prepare a place for us. It may not make sense at first, but the goal of every Christian is to keep heaven in heaven. Our laboring in Kingdom work should not be to make earth a suburb of heaven. God is calling us home and home is not here. Read Jesus' words about his purpose in returning to his father's house.

> [1] "Let not your hearts be troubled. Believe in God; believe also in me. [2] In my Father's house are many rooms. If it were not so, would I have told you that I go to prepare a place for you? [3] And if I go and prepare a place for you, I will come again and will take you to myself, that where I am you may be also." (John 14:1-3)

As the people of God, we have to align our priorities with his. We have to stop trying to do what was never a part of God's plan. Part of the problem may be we no longer know or even remember what Jesus wanted for his Church. This could very well be the central issue that has to be addressed. But, if it is, we have to find a way back to what Jesus taught the first disciples. The longer we wait to remove all the added baggage that has been added to our faith, the more difficult it will become. We are not the revolutionaries. Jesus is the revolutionary. We are simply and faithfully executing his plan.

Faith is more than something we do. It is someone we become. At the heart of the Gospel is a relationship with Jesus. Jesus is the reason we change. He is the one who calls us to greater obedience and dependence upon God. He is the one who teaches us how to live in a fallen world. He is the one who takes a wretched sinner and creates a saint of God. Only a savior like Jesus could do that.

The Gospel is the Call from Home

The power of faith to invigorate and transform must not be underestimated. As the Church, we have done so much damage to the Gospel. Not to the actual message but to the receptibility of it by those around us. The miracle is that in spite of our shortcomings God is able to redeem so many. The Gospel is powerful. The Gospel is the catalyst God created and uses to radically conform every person who believes into the image of Jesus.

The goal of the Church should be to foster and model faith-filled living, centered on the Gospel. The Gospel is the call from home. Whenever the Gospel is preached, discussed, and contemplated we are hearing the heart of God for his creation and his people. The power of the Gospel is not in the oratory or eloquence of the speaker but in the desire of the author. God himself proclaimed the Gospel to us in Jesus.

Carl Medearis in his book *Speaking of Jesus* makes a powerful case for the damage done by the church because of its subtle shift away from focusing exclusively and consistently on Jesus. Over the course of two thousand years, a few bad habits have snuck into the Church's understanding of herself. Medearis says that he is not trying to wage war on the Church or her doctrines. The issue, he contends, is all the baggage the Church has been carrying around.

> I don't want to redefine salvation. I don't want to redefine the gospel or even Christianity on the whole. I suppose I want to undefine them. I want to strip away the thousands of years of graffiti painted onto the gospel, turning it into a reasonable code of doctrines. The gospel is not an idea. It is not a belief. It is not a favorite verse. The gospel does not live in your church, it cannot be written down in a simple message, and it is not the sinner's prayer. The gospel is not a what. It is not a how. The gospel is a Who. The gospel is literally the good news of Jesus. Jesus is the gospel. [30]

This is a simple and yet profoundly difficult challenge. We have grown so accustomed to the way things are we do not take the time to consider if this is the way that it should be. Introspection has always been a part of the Christian experience. As a community, we must return to this practice. We must not shy away from making sure we understand what we are supposed to be doing as God's people. Each generation of believers must

---

[30] Carl Medearis, *Speaking of Jesus: The Art of Not-Evangelism* (Colorado Springs, CO: David C. Cook, 2011), 48.

make sure not to take anything for granted. We all have to discover the Gospel for ourselves.

One of the clearest indications we have departed from our commitment to journey toward home is failing to share what we have seen and heard. The Church's commitment to evangelism has ebbed and flowed throughout her history. As a pastor, I have found one of the areas many people struggle with is in personal evangelism. Most professing Christians would rather hide than engage anyone in a faith-centered conversation. Medearis' book again provides some helpful insight regarding this deficiency in evangelism. His perspective is as biting as it is helpful.

> Why is it so painful and embarrassing to share our faith? Because the gospel has become encumbered, handcuffed to traditions, movements, and organizations. Even handcuffed to society and government. To millions of people around the world, Jesus Christ is synonymous with Western society and America. The problem isn't that these attachments are or aren't good; the problem is that these things are not the gospel. Do we really want to try to redefine and reinterpret Jesus and then give Him to the world? Of course not. When we handcuff things to Jesus, we are convoluting the message. The power of Jesus' life and death come from His existence as the exact

representation of His Father. Do we really want to add to that?[31]

My hope is that we will stop talking about faith as something to hold or simply as principles that guide our lives, providing boundaries for our convictions. Faith is so much more than that. We must work harder to do what Jude admonished. Jude wanted to write about something else but felt compelled to write about the simplest of themes, the Gospel.

> [3] Beloved, when I gave all diligence to write unto you of the common salvation, it was needful for me to write unto you, and exhort you that ye should earnestly contend for the faith which was once delivered unto the saints. (Jude 3 KJV)

We exercise faith in Jesus because we see and have accepted the desperate nature of our lost-ness. We exercise faith in Jesus because we desire for our lives to become incarnations of Jesus in our contemporary context. To do any less is to deny what is plain to see, that trusting in Jesus means accepting our nature and our need for salvation.

We have looked at what faith is. Now it is time to accept that faith is not just what I do. Faith is who I have become because I have surrendered my life to Jesus. He is now living in and through me for God's glory and for the

---

[31] Ibid., 60.

sake of the mission of taking the Gospel to the ends of the earth. If I were to summarize what all this means it would be this: My desire is that every day I embody all that I believe so that God's glory and the Gospel of Jesus are seen more clearly in and through my life.

About the Author

Victor R. Scott currently serves as the Executive Pastor for Ministry Development and Discipleship at Ambassadors of Christ Ministries in Columbus, Georgia.

He graduated from Georgia Southern University his undergraduate degree and completed his Master of Divinity degree from Luther Rice University and Seminary.

Victor married his high school sweetheart and has two daughters who happen to share the same birthday.